ARROWS *of* TRUTH

A Strategy to Deflect Satan's Lies,
Embrace God's Truth, and Restore Your Mind

Debbie Gordon

Copyright © 2022 by Debbie Gordon

All rights reserved. This book or any portion thereof may not be reproduced or used in any matter whatsoever without the express written permission from the author except for the use of brief quotations in a book review.

All scripture quotations, unless otherwise indicated, are taken from the Holy Bible, New International Version ®, NIV®, Copyright © 1985.

Printed in the United States of America.

First printing 2022

Paperback ISBN: 978-1-7360103-2-7
Hardback ISBN: 978-1-7360103-3-4

Dedication

This book is dedicated to two pastors who profoundly blessed my life: Pastor Daniel and Pastor Leo. Both have taught me so much about spiritual warfare. They have reached into my life and supported my family and me through intercession. I am thankful for their ministries. I never dreamed that two African pastors would bless my heart so much. Thank you for teaching me how to pray authoritative prayers of power. And Pastor Daniel, thank you for your message that was the inspiration for this book.

Free Give Away

Affirmations are truths that help change the way we think. By placing these positive thoughts in our minds we can begin to counter the negative thoughts and negative things we say to ourselves. You can claim fifty Bible affirmations by going to the link found at:
https://godsaffirmations.com/affirmations.

Contents

	Preface	1
1.	Toxic Positivity	3
2.	Beginning Steps	6
3.	Removing Worry	8
4.	Voices of God	10
5.	Armor of God	22
6.	Arrows of Satan	25
7.	Bible Stories	28
8.	Stepping Out of Denial	37
9.	Gratitude	40
10.	Preventing Relapse	44
11.	Feelings and the Arrows of Truth	48
12.	Anger	55
13.	Anxiety	70
14.	Generosity	82
15.	Sadness	87
16.	Children of God	98
17.	Distance	109
18.	Hope	112
19.	Stress and Worry	117
	References	134

Preface

This book is not meant to be an exhaustive list for mental and emotional help. It is only one tool. It is not meant to diagnose issues. Instead, it is meant to be a source to steer you toward healing and wholeness. I am not making light of the issues and difficulties each of you may face. Change doesn't often happen instantaneously. Often, transformation and healing happen as we work the steps toward recovery. It is a process. Only God has the power to restore and heal us completely. As you read through this book, I hope it will help you begin the process with God's help.

Every emotion we face has both good and negative aspects. Don't discount any of them, though, because each one brings positive things into our lives. I hope that you will take time to puzzle through this concept and uncover both the good and negative things you experience with each emotion so that you can begin to reclaim the wholeness that God so desperately aches to give you.

It takes work to become whole. Open the doors you need to help you. This book is not meant to make light of the fact that maybe you will need the help of professionals. A need for professional guidance and support is totally okay. Each of us needs to open the necessary doors to help us recover. Let God guide you and help you as you grow and heal.

INTRODUCTION

As I discuss the emotions in this book, remember that they are not right or wrong. They just are feelings that you have. Try not to judge them as either good or bad. Identify the ones you have. As you work on healing and recovery you can begin to claim the opposite light emotions. You will begin to change and heal as God helps you reclaim these. This can only happen with God's power.

As we dive in, allow yourself to begin the process of uncovering the feelings that come up in your life. Ask God to help you. Allow yourself to feel the emotions. This may be challenging initially, but it will get easier in time. You will find parts of yourself returning. When we shut down our feelings, we also shut down pieces of ourselves, which does not allow us to be whole. God aches so much for you to become whole again. Allow God to help you uncover the parts of you that you have hidden away as you have tucked your feelings deep inside of you. He will help you change.

Blessings to each of you as you begin this exciting journey of discovery and healing.

← 1 →

Toxic Positivity

Toxic positivity happens when we don't validate the thoughts and feelings of others. It occurs when we don't listen to understand the experiences and emotions of others. Maybe we say things like, "Quote scriptures. Pray. Focus on the positives, and everything will get better. The situation will improve or resolve." I believe in prayer. I believe in scriptures, and I believe God cares. Healing happens instantaneously, gradually, or in heaven.

We are all different, and each situation is unique. When we use toxic positivity with people, it invalidates their feelings and makes them feel like their issue is not important or they aren't doing the right things—resolving their problems the right way. It minimizes their pain. They don't feel heard. It can turn people away from the church and away from a connection with God. Also, it makes people feel like feelings are wrong and that they must push all their feelings down and pretend they don't exist.

The reality is that our feelings are charge neutral. They are not right or wrong. They are emotions that well up inside us stemming from our experiences and thoughts. Pushing away these feelings suffocates parts of us. It doesn't allow us to be who we are. Additionally, pushing away all emotions only allows us to access some feelings. We become insensitive to the pain and suffering of others.

TOXIC POSITIVITY

It prevents us from being good listeners. We don't listen to hear. We listen with our own agenda, which is not healthy.

For years I attended a church where I was forced to put on a mask. That mask helped me pretend to others that I was okay when underneath, I was struggling deeply with sorrow, sadness, exhaustion, worries, stress, suicidal thoughts, anxiety, and more. The myriad of feelings inside of me were almost overwhelming. I was supposed to pretend I was okay, but this pretense ate away at the inside of me and almost destroyed me. When I finally walked away from this toxic church environment, I began to embrace the fact that it was okay not to be okay.

God helped me begin the process of recovery and healing. I began to realize that denial was a dangerous thing. It allowed the wounds inside to fester and become unhealthy. We can't heal an outside wound by pretending it's not there. What happens when we deny that we have an infected sore? It becomes worse. We can develop a dangerous infection that can kill us. The same is true on the inside of us. Denial is dangerous. It can cause the inside of us to fester and become unhealthy. This can lead to physical and mental illnesses.

Every emotion has a positive characteristic for us. Selfishness, at times, can be healthy as it allows us the opportunity to take care of ourselves so we can, in turn, care for others. Sadness allows us time to self-reflect and begin to process what triggered the emotion. Anger can help us understand that our boundaries are off. Pushing away or denying these feelings hurts us. We miss out on the positives that these feelings bring to our lives.

I will never forget the day I was wrestling with the pain that the editing process of my memoir uncovered as I prepared it for publication. Inside I was raw with the pain

TOXIC POSITIVITY

of grief. My heart and mind were hurting, but I decided to attend church. During that church service, I was told just to pray and claim scriptures, and then all the feelings from grief would go away. This angered me, and I countered the person who suggested these ideas. Three times I brought up stories to help shift this thinking. Yet, I was made to feel like I was wrong. Inside I hurt deeply and felt their callous, insensitive remarks wounded me more. In the end, I decided to step away from that group. It wasn't healthy. They minimized the pain of others, including my own. What I needed that day was for someone to listen to me and try to understand. Instead, I was unheard, and my thoughts were discounted.

Healing from our internal pain happens when our pain is heard and validated. We must not be afraid of our emotions and feelings. Every single one of them brings blessings to us. They all help us become the person we were intended to be.

I choose to embrace my feelings. They're reflections of my experiences. I no longer disown my emotions even upon the recommendation of others. I want to be whole. To be whole, it is time for me to embrace each emotion God has created. Each one has something to teach me, and I'm eager to embrace them all.

My prayer for each of you is that you will begin to embrace the fact that feelings are not right or wrong. They're all part of you, and it is perfectly okay not to be okay. I pray that each of you will embrace this and begin the process of internal reflection so that you can find the healing and peace you need in your lives. God aches for the inner pain inside of you to heal. May you find peace and sanity in your lives. May hope be restored to each of you.

← 2 →

Beginning Steps

Satan tries his hardest to attack our minds so he can control us and keep us down. This, then, prevents us from achieving the purpose, plan, and destiny God has for our lives. Satan knows the exact way to accomplish this task. He can bring thoughts from the past—regret, pain, suffering, shame, loss, negative things people have said to us over the years, stress, and more. It becomes a slippery slope.

He gradually works to fill our minds with these thoughts, and then he fuels us with lies—we are not appreciated, we are not loved, we are worthless, we are alone. These lies take on different thoughts for each of us, but we are all attacked and hammered by him. If we choose to listen to these thoughts, we can slowly slip into darkness and despair. Depression, hopelessness, pain, grief, and shame can then consume us.

But it is time for us to reclaim our lives, to redeem these thoughts by filling our minds with God's truth. God loves us. He promises never to leave us or forsake us. He assures us that we are a child of God. We are His. We were bought through His gift, the sacrifice of His life on the cross. Nothing at all will separate us from His love. It is time we reclaim our minds and begin filling our thoughts with truth. This book is meant to help each of us. May God begin to bring hope, peace, and sanity back into your lives. God

BEGINNING STEPS

aches to free each of us. It can only happen through the power of Jesus Christ.

← 3 →

Removing Worry

Years ago, I decided to stop listening to the news because it was filled with so much negativity. Negative stories were far more common than positive ones. I wanted to fill my mind with optimistic things rather than depressing things, so I quit watching it. At that period in my life, I struggled with a multitude of feelings caused by grief after my boyfriend drowned. I needed positivity, not negativity.

My daily struggle was real. Many days it felt like I was walking through a dark tunnel. I wondered if I would ever find the light again. I needed stories of hope, not stories of gloom and anxiety. I tried to fill my mind with stories like *Guideposts* offers so I could focus on good things. At night when I couldn't sleep, I'd listen to *Nightsounds*, a hope-filled radio program that plays late at night. During the day, I filled my mind with hymns, bible verses, prayer, and writing. The darkness slowly eased, and I eventually found the light again.

Depression and anxiety can creep into our lives from so many avenues. The COVID pandemic is a prime example of fear entering our lives. It was everywhere, filling us with dread and anxiousness. During this difficult period, I made a conscious effort to remove myself from social media because I heard stress, dread, anxiety, worries, and turmoil everywhere I turned. My work life was stressful enough as we were being pushed rapidly into the unknown world of

REMOVING WORRY

teletherapy. To add to this stress, I was struggling with my health, and COVID stress was taking a huge emotional toll on me. I had to focus on other things. So I removed myself from the pessimistic things that surrounded me and focused on writing, prayer, God, my family, Celebrate Recovery, and caring for a stray kitten brought into my life at the beginning of the pandemic. Focusing on these things caused me to regain my balance. Hope, sanity, and peace flowed back into my life.

The choice is ours. Are we going to listen to the world around us? The news and media fuel our anxiety and bring worry, fear, and concern into our lives. Instead, what if we focused on the peaceful and happy things happening in our lives? This is our daily choice. Do we want to be revved up or calmed down? My choice is to chisel out peace in every area of my life that I can. What about you?

What is causing your ship to sink, to be filled with terror, depression, negativity, hopelessness, anxiety, and fear? How can you right these feelings inside of you? Are there negative things you can remove from your life? Are there things you can add into your life that bring you peace?

The choice is yours. This book will guide you through these thoughts about what you can do to help right your ship.

― 4 ―

Voices of God

Over the years, I faced many emotions and continued to wrestle with grief. I realized, though, that the difficult feelings and pain I face are Satan's way of attacking and discouraging me so he can keep me down. When he keeps me down, I can't fulfill the work God has placed me on this earth to accomplish. We have a daily choice to focus on the positive voice of God that encourages us, fills us with hope, inspires us, and fills us with comfort, or to focus on the negative voice of Satan that condemns us, fills us with fear, discourages us, depresses us, makes us feel worthless, insecure, isolated, and alone. The choice is ours. Will we focus on the negative voice of Satan or the positive voice of God? Daily this is the choice we must make no matter the distractions, worries, anxiety, pain, and difficulties we face. Will we listen to God or to Satan?

We all have our challenges. Every one of us has things that we fight in our minds. Maybe it's insecurities or the belief that you aren't good enough, maybe it's depression or anxiety, maybe it's feelings of abandonment and rejection, maybe it's self-harm, maybe it's addictions to drugs and alcohol, maybe it's fear of people and new situations, or maybe it is memories of past abuse. The list is endless, but the reality is that all of us struggle with hurts, habits, and hang-ups. None of us are perfect, and the battles we fight inside us are real to each of us. Just getting up in the morning may be challenging, making it through the day may be difficult, panic attacks may hit you, gloominess may surround you, and stress may fill your life. Only you know what your challenges are.

My great aunt had a saying, "If we were to hang our troubles out on a line, you would take yours, and I would take mine." Although we all have challenges, we know how to work with them. Over the years, hopefully, we have learned positive ways to cope with them. Maybe we are still working on finding healthier coping strategies, but we know our issues, and when we look at the struggles others face, we realize that our issues are small in comparison. We all have struggles. I would not wish my challenges on anyone, nor would I ask God to give me other people's challenges. Mine are enough to bear. This is what this saying means. When we finally grasp the hurts, habits, hang-ups, and difficulties of others, we begin to see that our own problems are what we'd rather face.

God promises us that He will give us the power and strength to make it through each and every day. Daily He will provide us with the resources and help we need. Our job is to focus on trusting Him and asking Him for the help we need today. We weren't asked to face tomorrow. God tells us not to worry about tomorrow. Healthiness comes when we realize that we can only face today's challenges. The present is what our mind needs to focus on. Our job needs to keep the past in the past and the future in the future. This can only happen as we embrace God and ask Him to help us.

Thinking about this concept reminds me of a really tough day I had a few years ago. Suddenly, profoundly deep dark thoughts enveloped me, filling me with pain, overwhelming my entire mind. The darkness was so thick that I could slice it with a knife. It took over me and covered me like a blanket, almost suffocating me. These deep dark thoughts plagued my mind and filled me with such intense pain that I wasn't sure I could bear any more. Peace was suddenly gone from my mind, and all that remained was blackness and anguish.

I sat trying everything I could to push through this very difficult moment as Satan tried everything in his power to discourage and oppress me and encourage me to rely on unhelpful strategies that I'd used in the past. But I fought back, determined not to return to those old useless strategies. I hadn't done them for months. Why would I go back to them again?

So I sat on my bed listening to hymns, praying, crying, and asking God to help me with this deep pain and suffering. It seemed like an eternity that I sat there crying, consumed by the darkest thoughts imaginable. I wished I could sleep, but I couldn't because my mind was oppressed by the ugliest thoughts. I did everything in my power to refrain from the temptations that tormented my mind. I cried out to God for support and asked God to raise my name to people's minds so they would pray for me.

Immediately, peace came over me, and I fell into a deep slumber. The oppression was gone, the darkness had been pushed away, the evil had been asked to leave, and I could breathe and think again.

The Bible says in I Peter 5:8, "Your enemy the devil prowls around like a roaring lion looking for someone to devour." But when we cry out to God, rebuke Satan, and ask God for help, God promises to help us. He pushes back the devil and causes the oppression to leave.

Satan is out to attack us. Daily he works out plans to tear us down, destroy us, hurt us, tempt us, and throw arrows

VOICES OF GOD

at us to attack our minds. How do we manage these attacks?

We must focus on today.

Here is another story to help you realize the importance of thinking about today, focusing on the challenges in front of you, asking God to help you with the daily needs you have, and taking your day one step at a time. I will take you back to another difficult day in my life where I realized the incredible importance of focusing on the present.

In the *Lord of the Rings*, the trip to Mordor, taken by Frodo and his friends, has been firmly etched in my mind as I once walked along that same grim, dark, gloomy road. I felt a thick blackness as I journeyed down that road and relived memories that I thought I had long forgotten. But somehow, those memories were pulled out and resurfaced in my mind.

The eyes of Golem gleamed at me, reminding me that my desires would do no good, as he had the power to threaten and torment my mind no matter my desire for peace. Indeed, I found no peace as I traveled down this lonely road. I cried out to God, begging for this journey to Mordor to end. It is the most solitary road anyone could ever travel down. All that surrounded me were the gleaming eyes of Golem and darkness so thick and heavy that it almost suffocated me. Poor dear Frodo, in his journey to save his friends, understood this difficult road.

But Jesus also understands this path of pain. He had to carry His own cross that He was crucified on. The darkness and sorrow Jesus faced are no different than what I have faced. He understands my pain and suffering that were depicted so amazingly in J.R.R Tolkien's books and in the story of the crucifixion of Jesus. The heaviness, pain, and suffering of these journeys are things that we may face here on this earth. We may need to push through tough and difficult days on this earth, but Jesus' crucifixion reminds us that God will win in the end. Just as Frodo won on his journey, we, too, will win as well because Jesus went before us and paved the road for us to have victory.

Some days it takes lots of prayer to make it through the day. That day was one of those days. I asked God for help. I received it. And then God provided a reminder to me in the form of a crescent moon that was like a cradle in the sky. As I stared up at it, God reminded me that He was there, ready to hold me in his arms, place me in my bed and allow me to rest while He rocked me to sleep and comforted me. He is a God who knows exactly what we need exactly when we need it most.

Each of us may experience Mordor days in our lives where it takes everything in our power to fight the devil and make it through the day. Cry out to God and reach out to friends for help. God is with us all the way, and He will cause us to be victorious. With Him, we will have the strength, power, and help we need to make it through. He will provide the armor we need to succeed and thwart the devil. We will be victorious. God will win. May we never lose heart.

Maybe you can relate to this next story. Grief sent me into a terrible tailspin. My life felt hopeless and gloomy. Darkness consumed me, and grief clung to every part of my being. I was simply going through the motions of living. Inside I was hurting deeply and felt there was no reason to live again. Pain filled every part of my being. I felt alone, isolated, and abandoned. One night the negative thoughts in my mind, depression, darkness, hopelessness, grief, gloom, and despair, consumed my mind. I couldn't handle it anymore and tried to take my life.

VOICES OF GOD

But at that moment, God met me and held me in His arms. He comforted me, encouraged me, and held me while I cried. He filled my mind with a purpose that kept me going during one of the darkest times in my life. God prompted me to write. When I could not sleep and felt discouraged, I began to write my first book. It became the thing that kept me going. I woke up each day eager to share more. The book grew, and within a few months, I had finished the story—my book, *Legacy of Love: Lessons in Love, Loss, and Recovery*. From that point on, writing became the thing that kept me going. It was the driving force of my life. I had a purpose.

As I share these words, I pray that we all will be more aware of Satan and his tactics. God gives us peace, joy, assurance, love, and hope. These positive things are what we need to remember and hold onto each and every day. When we feel discouraged, sad, burdened, and gloominess overcoming us, we can be assured that these things come from Satan. We can ask God to rebuke Satan in the name of Jesus Christ, and we can ask God to surround us with His presence. God hears these prayers and is eager to help us when we are oppressed by the evil one. May we learn to cry out to God for the support and help we need. God is always there to hear our prayers.

Maybe you, too, suffer from some of these feelings and thoughts. You are not alone. These thoughts can take us down, but remember that they are also thrown at us by Satan to discourage us and tempt us to give up. We cannot listen to these thoughts. We need to learn to diffuse these thoughts with positive messages and truth from the Bible through our own prayer and asking others to pray for us.

This life has not been easy, and grief has not been the only difficult feeling I have experienced. A myriad of other challenging emotions have pushed me to the edge at times. Pain arising from difficult experiences has consumed me sometimes, and Satan has tried his best to keep me down and discouraged, preventing me from achieving God's plans for my life. But God began to speak to me and teach me things.

One day when feeling alone, dejected, depressed, anxious, worthless, insecure, and upset, God spoke to me, saying, "The feelings you are having are because of abandonment." Suddenly image after image began to race through my mind. My biological father's lack of involvement in my life, my boyfriend drowning, the disconnectedness of my family, lack of acceptance, love, and support at church, and more. At that moment, I understood why I felt the way I did. All these feelings and thoughts could be traced to one word—abandonment. Then God opened doors for me to attend Celebrate Recovery and begin the process of healing. It was the beginning of finding connections, love, and support. Slowly, I began to heal.

I share these thoughts because I ache for you to find healing and hope as well. We all face hurts and challenges in this life. Pain happens in so many ways. My pain is different from your pain, but we all have experienced things that have about destroyed us. I want to encourage you to recognize that you are not alone.

What are you feeling today? Where does that feeling come from? I want you to focus on these things. Explore your feelings. Identify all of them. Why are you feeling that way? Be specific. What memories cause these feelings? Bring this pain to God. Pray about this pain and ask God to help you heal. Then begin taking these negative thoughts and attaching positive thoughts to them by claiming

VOICES OF GOD

scripture verses. When negative thoughts come up, pray and ask God to help you. Repeat positive Bible verses you have written down. To overcome negativity, you must fill your mind with positivity. We do this by praising God, singing, listening to Christian music, reading scripture, writing, drawing, spending time in nature, reaching out to friends or accountability partners, and filling our minds with positive thoughts and scriptures. With practice and with God's help, you will begin to fill your mind with positive voices and thoughts that come from God rather than the negative ones.

Prayer is the key. This is how I see prayer working. See my diagram below:

```
                    God
                God God God
            God God God God God
         God Satan   Satan   Satan God
        God Satan               Satan God
       God Satan      US        Satan God
        God Satan              Satan God
         God Satan   Satan   Satan God
            God God God God God
                God God God
                    God
```

VOICES OF GOD

When we pray, this is what happens:

```
            Satan   Satan   Satan
         Satan  God   God   God  Satan
       Satan  God  God  God  God  Satan
     Satan  God  God  God  God  God  Satan
   Satan  God  God              God  God  Satan
   Satan  God  God      US      God  God  Satan
   Satan  God  God              God  God  Satan
     Satan  God  God  God  God  God  Satan
       Satan  God  God  God  God  Satan
         Satan  God  God  God  Satan
            Satan   Satan   Satan
```

Remember the story of Jesus found in Matthew 4 when He was led to the wilderness and tempted for forty days and forty nights? He faced all kinds of temptations by Satan. Three times He was tempted, but every time Jesus responded to the temptations with scriptures and words of truth.

This is the key for us. To withstand these temptations and lies, we must gird ourselves with truth. This is where the scripture comes in. We must refute these negative thoughts with scriptures of truth. These are what I will call arrows of truth. So when we are told, "you are worthless and unworthy," you refute this with truth from the scriptures.

God says we are valuable. Matthew 6:26 says, "Look at the birds of the air; they do not sow or reap or store away in barns, and yet your heavenly Father feeds them. Are you not much more valuable than they are?" Isaiah 43:4 says, "You are precious and honored in God's sight." Luke 12:7 says, "Even the hairs of your head are numbered. You are more valuable than many sparrows. Psalm 139:13-16 says, "God created your inmost being; He knit you together in my mother's womb. Praise God because you are fearfully and wonderfully made. His works are wonderful, I know that full well. Your frame was not hidden from Him when you were made in the secret place. When you were woven together in the depths of the earth, His eyes saw my unformed body. All the days ordained for me were written in your book before one of them came to me."

Satan tries his hardest to fill our minds with negativity and lies. Remember the story of Adam and Eve? What did they do? In Genesis 3:1, it says that the serpent questioned Eve, "Did God really say, 'You must not eat from any tree in the garden?' The woman said to the serpent, 'We may eat fruit from the trees in the garden, but God did say, You must not eat fruit from the tree that is in the middle of the garden, and you must not touch it, or you will die.'"

Keep reading on. As you read, you realize that Satan distorted the truth. He does the same to us. He told Eve that she would not die but that she would have an understanding of good and evil.

It was true that Adam and Eve wouldn't die that day, but their action of taking the fruit God asked them not to take did harm their lives. They did eventually die, so what

VOICES OF GOD

Satan said was not true. He lied to them as he does to us as well.

The voice of Satan speaks doubt, shame, confusion, fear, anxiety, despair, rage, embarrassment, hopelessness, loneliness, regret, remorse, and worry. All of the negative emotions listed in this book stem from Satan. We need to stop listening to these voices and thoughts and begin to fill our minds with the positive voice of God and the positive feelings God aches to give us. This is how we begin our battle plan. We begin to focus on the arrows of truth, the positive voices, the positive thoughts.

How do we do this? We do this by writing down the negative emotions we are thinking about and finding reasons for feeling these things. Do these feelings come from past mistakes or past experiences? Do we fear the future? Once we find the root of these feelings and thoughts, then we must begin to push away the fiery arrows of negative emotions. We do this by digging into the Bible. What does God say? Keep asking yourself this question. Search for the truths from the Bible. Memorize and claim these truths. Write them down on index cards so you can refer to them when you are faced with these negative emotions. Fill your minds with the positive truths.

God says in Matthew 10:31, "Fear not, therefore; you are of more value than many sparrows." The Bible verses are our arrows of truth. Satan fuels our minds with the arrows of lies, doubt, pain, and anguish. We refute these fiery arrows with God's arrows of truth found in the Bible. Filling our minds with the truth deflates Satan's attack on our minds.

What arrows of lies does Satan attack you with? Is it that you aren't good enough? Is it shame from the past? Is it grief? Is it abandonment or rejection? Is it guilt? Identify all your triggers. Then make a plan to deflect them with truth from the Bible.

← 5 →

Armor of God

When we think of war, we think of armor. Protection is important in war. Over the years, many types of armor have been developed to deflect arrows, bullets, and other weapons of war. This is important to ensure that fewer losses happen. As Christians, we all face war every day of our lives. The mission of Satan from the time of our conception is to steal, kill, and destroy us. He is a master of destruction and does everything in his power to deter us from the mission God has placed us on this earth to complete. He sabotages us, discourages us, tears us down, makes us worry, fills us with self-doubt, and prevents us from accomplishing the work God has designed for us to do.

Thinking about this war reminds me of the story of Nehemiah. When Nehemiah learned that his fellow Israelites were struggling to repair their city after enemies ravaged it, he was saddened. His boss, the king, saw his discouragement and asked him what was wrong. When Nehemiah told him, the king told him to go and help his nation. The king even said that he would provide the resources for Nehemiah to return home and help his country. So Nehemiah returned to his homeland.

But the story is one of struggle and difficulty. Every way he turned, Nehemiah was attacked. People were angry that the Israelites were rebuilding their city, and they were out to attack them every way they could. It got to the point

ARMOR OF GOD

where the people had to work with a sword in one hand to protect themselves as they worked to rebuild the city with the other hand. The Israelites continued to be attacked, but Nehemiah did not give up. Instead, he continued to organize the Israelites and give them assignments. He gave them the courage to rebuild the wall that would protect their city from their enemies. It wasn't an easy job, but they persevered. With effort and determination, the task was eventually finished.

As a single parent, I felt like Nehemiah. I felt everyone constantly attacked me. Church should have been a place of solace. Instead, it felt like a place where nobody wanted me. I was the black sheep; I was the misfit. I felt unwanted, unappreciated, and unloved. The trials I faced seemed impossible. My life was challenging, but I didn't give up. I continued to persevere despite the fiery darts that flew all around me.

We are all in a war. Your war is different than my war, but it is war nonetheless. To survive, we must clothe ourselves with armor. Ephesians 6:10-18 tells us how to do this. It says, "Finally, be strong in the Lord and in His mighty power. Put on the full armor of God so that you can take your stand against the devil's schemes. For our struggle is not against flesh and blood, but against the rulers, against the authorities, against the powers of this dark world, and against the spiritual forces of evil in the heavenly realms. Therefore, put on the full armor of God so that when the day of evil comes, you may be able to stand your ground, and after you have done everything, to stand. Stand firm then, with the belt of truth buckled around your waist, with the breastplate of righteousness in place, and with your feet fitted with the readiness that comes from the gospel of peace. In addition to all this, take

ARMOR OF GOD

up the shield of faith, with which you can extinguish all the flaming arrows of the evil one. Take the helmet of salvation and the sword of the Spirit, which is the word of God."

Putting on the armor of God is a powerful way to refute the arrows and attacks of Satan. How do we do this? Before I enter into my ministry, I take time to pray with God and connect with Him. I spend time in His word. Then I pray through this text, asking God to put His armor on me. I specifically go through all of it and say to God, "Place your belt of truth around my waist, cover me with the breastplate of righteousness, shod my feet with the gospel of peace, and provide me with the shield of faith so I can extinguish the flaming arrows of the evil one and give me the helmet of salvation and the sword of the Spirit which is the word of God." I visualize God providing all of this armor for me. I pray for Him to also make the words of my mouth and the meditations of my heart acceptable in His sight. I ask Him to help my mouth, my eyes, my ears, my hands, and my feet be His instruments that He will use to bless and encourage others.

←─ 6 ─→

Arrows of Satan

Satan is out to kill, steal and destroy us every way he can. We must remain connected to God. When we submit our lives to God, have our daily quiet time with God, and fill our minds with scriptures, this helps us thwart the devil's attacks. Satan tries to destroy our minds in every way he can. He does this by attacking us. His darts of negativity and his negative thoughts will permeate our minds if we allow them to. We need to keep alert to these attacks and be aware. Some signs that our minds are under spiritual attack are:

1. Negative/Pessimistic Thoughts
2. Distracted/Unable to Focus
3. Difficulty Praying
4. Falling Asleep During Quiet Time With God
5. Depression/Anxiety/Seeing and Hearing Things (Mental Health Issues)
6. Self-Centered/Self-Focused
7. Obsessive Thoughts
8. Suicidal Thoughts/Hopelessness
9. Addictions/Compulsive Behaviors
10. Personality Changes

We need to develop a strategy to ward off these attacks. The most important thing is for us to deepen our relationship with God. We need to have a daily quiet time

ARROWS OF SATAN

with God in which we read the Bible and pray. We also need to find ways to fill ourselves with positive messages about God throughout our day and night. For example, when we feel lonely, we can remind ourselves of Deuteronomy 31:6, which says, "He will never leave us nor forsake us." Fill your mind with the truth to counteract the lies that others and Satan have told you. If you were told you were worthless, claim Luke 12:7, which says, "Indeed even the hairs of your head are all numbered. Don't be afraid; you are worth more than many sparrows." Maybe you are struggling with financial worries. Then claim Philippians 4:19, which says, "And my God will meet all your needs according to His glorious riches in Christ Jesus." For every issue we face, we must fill our minds with truth.

After you deepen your relationship with God, you need to identify the feelings and thoughts Satan attacks you with. Think about what they stem from as well. Be specific. Jot down all of the feelings and thoughts you struggle with and the reasons for these feelings. What situations in your life cause them? Write this down. Then attach a scripture to these feelings and thoughts that remind you of positive thoughts. This way, when Satan attacks you, you can defend yourself.

Positive thoughts will also help you see through the false words thrown at you. In the chapters following Feelings and the Arrows of Truth, you will find a selection of feelings, and you can see if they apply to you. Don't be afraid to add to the list if you need to. God will impress on your mind why you feel the way you do if you ask Him. The goal is to become aware of your triggers. What causes you to think negative thoughts? What lies does Satan fill your mind with? When you answer these questions, then you will create a battle plan that is right for you.

← 7 →

Bible Stories

Let's turn in our Bibles and begin looking at stories about Bible characters. I like these stories because they're about real people just like us who struggle and sin, but repeatedly God shows His love and mercy.

John 8:1-11 tells the story of an event that happened while Jesus was teaching the people. The scripture tells us that teachers of the law and Pharisees brought a woman caught in adultery to the place where Jesus was. Then they said to Jesus, "This woman was caught in the act of adultery. In the law, Moses commands us to stone such a woman. Now, what do you say?"

This must have been a terribly embarrassing situation for this woman. I envision a woman clothed in no more than a sheet surrounding her body. Why didn't they bring the man with her? They both sinned? But in this story, only the woman was brought before Jesus.

Their goal was to trap Jesus. However, Jesus remained calm. I'm sure He was praying and asking God for advice.

He said nothing at all. Instead, He bent down and started writing on the dust of the ground with His finger.

They continued to question Him as He wrote.

Finally, He straightened up and said, "If any of you is without sin, let him be the first to throw a stone at her." Then He again began writing on the ground.

I imagine the scene. Those proud, arrogant Pharisees and teachers of the law felt they were free of sin because they adhered to the law of Moses. But all humans on this earth sin. I imagine that Jesus began writing their sins down. Johab: judgementalism, negativity, lustfulness. Harrison: pride, sexual impurity. Jude: self-centeredness, stinginess, anger. Farso: slothfulness, greed. Jonadab: pride, jealousy, and so on.

Everyone who took part in bringing the woman to Jesus slowly began to leave as Jesus continued writing in the dirt. Eventually, He was left with only the woman. Jesus straightened up and, looking at the woman, He said, "Woman, where are your accusers? Has anyone condemned you?"

"No one, sir," she said.

"Then neither do I condemn you," Jesus declared. "Go and sin no more."

I can just imagine the relief on the woman's face as she realized that she was free. I'm certain that this event changed her life forever as well.

This story contains so many emotions. Let's start to pick them apart. The woman must have felt totally embarrassed, humiliated, and angry at the people who brought her to Jesus. She probably also felt shame and remorse. The teachers of the law felt prideful, arrogant, self-righteous, and free of sin. They were in total denial that they, too, were imperfect. They wore a mask of perfection and righteousness, which was just as much a sin as the adulterous situation. They are just different colored sins, as a friend of mine says.

What I like about this story is that Jesus shows us that He will forgive our sins. He loves us despite our sin. He desires to have a relationship with us and to restore our lives to sanity.

BIBLE STORIES

Then there is the story of Mary Magdalene. I love this story too. Mary had seven demons that Jesus cast out of her, and she and a group of women spent time aiding Jesus financially in His ministry. Luke 7:36 tells the story of Jesus being invited to a dinner at a Pharisee's home. He was reclining at the table, as was the custom of the day, when a woman—who had once lived a very sinful life until Jesus healed her—arrived bringing an alabaster jar of perfume. She stood at His feet weeping, wetting His feet with her tears. Then she wiped His feet with her long hair and began kissing his feet. I'm sure quite an audience of people watched this unusual scene. She opened the alabaster jar and poured the perfume all over Jesus' feet. I'm sure the fragrance of that perfume filled the home.

But there is always criticism with every action that we do. Good or bad, we will always be surrounded by critics. Our job must be to please God, not people.

The value of alabaster perfume was a year's wage back in Bible times. That is a lot of money. This woman must have had a business or a way to earn a significant amount of money to afford to buy this jar of perfume.

This thought brought a lot of negative comments. "Wouldn't it have been better for her to spend that money on the poor?" Judas Iscariot asked, thinking about the disciples' money to which he freely helped himself.

"It was intended that she should save this perfume for the day of my burial. You will always have the poor among you, but you will not always have me." Jesus replied.

Simon said, "If you were a prophet, you would know that the person touching you is a woman of tremendous sin."

As Jesus often did, He chose not to respond to the statement directly. Instead, he told a story, a parable, "Two men owed money to a money lender. One man owed him five hundred denarii, and the other man owed fifty. Neither man had the money to pay him back. So the man kindly canceled the debts of both of them. Now which of them will love him more?"

"Probably the man who had the bigger debt canceled," Simon replied.

"You have answered correctly," Jesus said.

Then turning to the woman, he said to Simon, "Do you see this woman? I came into your house. You did not give me water for my feet, but she wet my feet with her tears and wiped them with her hair. You did not give me a kiss, but this woman has not stopped kissing my feet from the time she entered the room. You did not pour oil on my head, but she poured perfume on my feet. Therefore, I tell you, her many sins have been forgiven, for she loved much. But he who has been forgiven little loves little."

Turning to the woman, Jesus said, "Your sins are forgiven. Your faith has saved you; go in peace."

Let's dissect the many emotions and feelings that occurred that day. Mary felt remorse, guilt, shame, broken, regret, sorrow, anguish. Maybe you can think of more feelings. If so, add them to the list. Simon felt disgust, anger, pride, negativity, judgment. Judas Iscariot felt anger, greed, self-centered thoughts, pride.

Keep thinking and puzzling through the feelings that may have occurred that day. Identifying the emotions in the story will help you identify your own feelings. What happened after Jesus shared the truth of His love for sinners just like Mary? Imagine the feelings she had then peace, joy, happiness, feelings of being loved and appreciated, hope. Keep adding to the list. There are no wrong answers. We will all see different things.

BIBLE STORIES

Let's keep going. Remember the stories about the lepers in the Bible. The lepers were the outcasts of society. They were viewed as unclean. Their illness prevented them from being with their families. They were isolated, alone, rejected, humiliated. Maybe you have felt these feelings. What other feelings do you imagine the lepers felt? Add them to the list. Can you imagine having to ring a bell no matter where you went to keep people away? Have you ever felt similar feelings? I know I have.

I was the black sheep at church as a single parent and felt rejected, unappreciated, and unaccepted. How about you? In life, have you faced these feelings? Write down these situations in a journal. How did it make you feel? The amazing thing is that God enters this scene, this pain, this sorrow. And He doesn't just enter this place of uncleanness. He does even more. He touches the lepers. "Be clean," He tells them. "Go to the priest and let Him declare that you are healed."

Now imagine what the lepers feel when Jesus enters the scene and heals them. They feel love, acceptance, appreciation, joy, hope, peace. Keep adding to the list. Remember, there are no wrong answers.

What about you? When God enters your life and heals you and removes these feelings from you, how do you feel? Think about this. Write it down. When God finally removed me from an unhealthy church where I felt unloved, unappreciated, and unaccepted, He carried me in His arms and dropped me into a support system called, Celebrate Recovery, where I finally felt loved, appreciated, and accepted. I finally found hope, joy, peace, and sanity. God began to work in my life to heal me. I want you to think about this. Healing is possible, but it can only happen through the power of Jesus.

BIBLE STORIES

What about the story of Joseph? He was loved and appreciated by his father. But his position of favor made his brothers jealous. Their jealousy and envy eventually led them to strip off the fine multi-colored robe their father had made and throw him into a pit. Imagine how Joseph felt. Think about it. Write it down. I imagine he felt sorrow and rejection. Keep adding to the list. He was eventually sold to the Ishmaelites and then sold to Potipher. The story does not end there. Potipher's wife had lustful thoughts. She kept trying to get Joseph to go to bed with her, but Joseph refused, knowing it was wrong. One day when he was alone with her, she trapped him. To escape, he had to leave his robe behind. Potipher's wife told her husband that Joseph had tried to attack her, so Joseph was imprisoned. How do you think that made Joseph feel? Write down the feelings. How would this make you feel? Has this ever happened to you?

Joseph was eventually freed from prison when the person in charge realized his character, but he couldn't leave prison. Instead, he was asked to be a leader and serve and help the prisoners. Well, he eventually had the opportunity to listen to the dreams of two prisoners. God had filled Joseph with wisdom, understanding, and the ability to interpret dreams. So he interpreted these men's dreams. Then he told the men to remember him and let Pharaoh know to be released from prison. This didn't happen immediately, though, because these men forgot about Joseph.

But God is always ready to help us even when we are in difficult situations, as Joseph was. In His time and perfect way, He works out amazing solutions in our lives. Joseph was asked to interpret Pharaoh's dream. He told Pharaoh there would be seven years of plenty and seven years of

BIBLE STORIES

famine. He advised that during the seven years of plenty, grain be put away and stored in Egypt. Pharaoh noticed Joseph's wisdom, and he raised Joseph up to be second in command of Egypt. Wow, did you hear that? Joseph literally went from prison to being a prime minister of Egypt. Can you imagine how Joseph felt?

The story continues to say that Joseph's brothers came to Egypt asking for grain, and Joseph gave it to them, but he also tested his brothers to see if they had changed. Eventually, he revealed who he was to his brothers. And the Bible says that Joseph wept. His brothers felt remorse, fear, and shame for their actions. But Joseph, just like God, extended forgiveness to his brothers. "What you intended for evil, God meant for good," Joseph told his brothers. Where have you been granted forgiveness in your lives? Think about these things and write them down. How did that make you feel? Are there any other areas in your life where you need to ask for forgiveness? Think about what those amends should look like for you.

I love the story of Elijah. Remember how rain did not fall in Israel at one point because the Israelites had turned away from God? There was little food during this time of no rain, and Israel suffered. But God worked in Elijah's life. He sent Elijah to the brook Cherith, where he was fed daily by the ravens. He had water and food. God provided for His needs. What an amazing time that must have been for Elijah. It was a daily reminder that God loved Elijah and would provide for his daily needs. But because there was no rain, the brook Cherith eventually dried up, and God had to send Elijah away. He was sent to the home of a widow and her son. The story tells us that the widow gathered sticks to prepare her last meal for herself and her son. God knew.

BIBLE STORIES

"Would you make food for me?" Elijah asked, not knowing the widow's plight.

What would you have done in this situation? Would you have made a meal for Elijah?

She had food only for only one meal, but this woman had a giving, kind heart. She made the meal for Elijah, knowing that this meant she would have no more food for herself or her son. Would you have done this?

The story tells us that she provided a place for Elijah to stay and her flour and oil never ran out. God blessed her because of her faith and kindness. I get goosebumps thinking about this story. If God could provide for Elijah and this widow, don't you think He can provide for our needs as well?

What areas of your life are you struggling with? Where do you need to ask God for determination? For me, it was the twenty-eight-year journey of writing my first book. What about you? May God fill you with the courage and persistence to continue the work you were called to do.

Then there is the story of Achan. The Israelites were asked to attack the cities around them and destroy the people and the cities. God told them not to bring any items back from this attack. But we are told that one man, Achan, coveted what he saw, and he took some items and hid them in the ground underneath his tent. He thought he could get away with it. But God saw what Achan did as He sees what each of us do. The Israelites lost their next battle. So Joshua went before God, asking God what happened. "Someone took items they were asked not to take. Cast lots, and I will show you who it is."

So Israel did this, and we are told that the lot fell of Achan and his family. That day Achan and all of his family were destroyed. God wanted the Israelites to follow what

BIBLE STORIES

He told them to do. What has God asked you to do? Have you listened to Him? What were the consequences of your actions? Blessings always happen to us when we follow God's will.

Judas Iscariot was a man of greed and self-centeredness. Yet, Jesus still allowed him to be one of His disciples. Being God, I have to believe that Jesus knew that Judas was stealing from their money as the treasurer of the disciples' money. But He said nothing. Instead, He continued to allow him to be a disciple. Eventually, the greed got to Judas. He turned Jesus into the Pharisees for thirty pieces of silver. Jesus knew this, and yet He still humbly washed Judas' feet. Would you have done this?

Jesus was eventually tried before the Romans and hung on a cross. There are so many thoughts to unpack with this story. We are told that Judas eventually killed himself. Think about the feelings and thoughts of Judas, of the disciples, and of Jesus during this time. Much can be thought about in this story. Write it down in your journal. If Jesus could be so kind to Judas and still wash his feet knowing what he was up to, what does this tell us about us? How will He respond to us and our sins? Does He still love us despite our sins? The answer is absolutely.

And we are told that He died on a cross to save us from our sins. Did you hear that? He died for each and every one of us despite our sinfulness. He loves us so much that He aches to reach into our pain, our brokenness, our remorse, our sins, our shame, and so on and bring healing and restoration to us. God loves us! And the Bible tells us that nothing can separate us from the love of God. Do you believe this? If not, ask God to help you believe this truth. He aches to free you and to heal you.

← 8 →

Stepping Out of Denial

Amid difficulties in life, with anxiety all around us, how do we find gratitude? For weeks I grappled with this question as the panic and stress of the pandemic's reactions surrounded us. It impacted all of us—our children's lives, financially, in stores, in restaurants, in our medical communities, in our educational systems, in our sporting events, and in our recreation. Maybe you felt like I did, okay, trusting God, but suddenly the stress and insanity of everyone and everything took its toll on you, and the slip into isolation and social distancing removed strongholds to help you.

Face-to-face meetings were removed, social gatherings were stripped away, and peace was suddenly gone. All I know is that one minute I was grounded, encouraging others to focus on God, not on the fear around them, and the next, my asthma took a turn for the worse. I found myself in the emergency room doing breathing treatments to restabilize. I received medications, but the isolation caused my abandonment issues to escalate. Stress caused my anxiety to escalate, and we were thrown into unknown terrain.

The medication I received caused me to struggle emotionally. Suddenly, I was in a downward spiral. It was like I'd stepped into the quicksand, and I was rapidly sinking downward. I snapped. I was beginning to crack and knew that I had to ask for time off work. Thankfully, my supervisors agreed. By that point, I could hardly finish wrapping up all that needed to be done. I began praying and watched as my schedulers stepped in to help me. When I could not go on any longer, God made a way. The next day I received a text telling me that my second job was canceled for the remainder of the school year. I watched as God literally freed my schedule. But depression and anxiety worked their way into my mind as Satan continued attacking me. Isolation left me vulnerable, and I began struggling.

Maybe you've been there. You are standing firm one minute and suddenly find yourself slipping. What should you do? What are the steps you need to take?

The first step is stepping out of denial and facing our issues. For me, my conversation with myself went something like this, "I am feeling anxious about all the changes at work. Isolation isn't helping. The fear around me isn't helping. I must face that I am struggling and do something."

Your first step is to face what you are dealing with. Are there addictions that you are struggling with? Is your mental health challenging right now? Are there obsessive thoughts that you are having? Is depression taking hold of you? Are there relationship challenges that are making your life difficult? Identify what is bothering you. This is how you step out of denial. Then develop an action plan.

I'll share my action plan with you. I began talking to God about my anxiety and depression, and I began to seek His help for a solution. I also reached out to my doctor and told him about my struggles. Then I reached out to my accountability team and asked for prayer. After stepping out of denial, we must take our challenges to God. He is the only one that can help us change. He always has a perfect solution for our problems.

In a dark pit of despair, it can be difficult to find an attitude of gratitude. In the pandemic, we were isolated and unable to do the things we normally did. It can be hard to see things to be thankful for. But even in the midst of our difficulties and turmoil in our country, we must focus on our daily quiet time with God and have Him help us have an attitude of gratitude. We must look around us and find things to be thankful for—sunshine, beautiful weather, staying connected via Zoom, texts, and phone calls. We are alive, God is still in control, we have cars, we have a place to live, and we have hope because God is in control of our nation, community, and world. He is the true king of this world. Our job is to look up to God, focus on Him, and remain positive. There is always something to be thankful for.

Praising God is so important in our recoveries. When we praise God, victories happen!

← 9 →

Gratitude

Have you heard about keeping a gratitude journal? This is a journal where we record things that we are thankful for. Doing this helps us focus on positive things rather than on anxiety, fear, worry, anger, sadness, panic and grief, and the many other emotions surrounding us. The pandemic created a rollercoaster of emotions. Yet, I believe more than ever that when we face so much stress and unrest, we must learn to praise and thank God. Gratitude is super important. But how can we praise God in the middle of our difficulties?

As I think about this question, I am reminded of when I attended a co-worker's funeral. When my children and I opened the doors of the sanctuary, we witnessed a large choir singing happy, joyful music. People danced in the aisle of the church. It was so different from the somber, serious funerals I was used to attending. These people were dancing and singing during a time of grief and sorrow. We left that "fun-eral," laughing and happy despite the loss of my coworker.

Acts 16:16-40 shares the story of a demon-possessed slave girl that earned a great deal of money for her owners by fortune-telling. When Paul began to preach to the people of the area, the girl continued shouting, "These men are servants of the most-High God, who are telling you the way to be saved."

GRATITUDE

She must have been quite a distraction because Paul got annoyed and angry and finally said to the spirit, "In the name of Jesus Christ, I command you to come out of her!"

According to the Bible, at that moment the spirit left her. But the slave girl's owners were furious because they'd lost their income, so they seized Paul and Silas and dragged them to the magistrates.

"These men are Jews," they said. "They are throwing this city into an uproar by advocating customs unlawful for us Romans to accept or practice."

The magistrate ordered that Paul and Silas be beaten, thrown into prison, and their feet placed into stocks. The day couldn't have gone much worse for Paul and Silas, and they must have been in physical pain from the flogging and confinement of the stocks. Yet, at midnight despite the challenges and difficulties they faced, Paul and Silas began praying and singing hymns while the other prisoners were listening. They chose to praise God despite their circumstances.

Wow! Even when life was the pits, they found a way to praise God. God heard them and must have been thrilled because suddenly, a violent earthquake shook the foundations of the prison, and all at once, the prison doors flew open, and everyone's chains came loose. Did you catch that? Praising God in spite of our difficulties causes miracles to happen in our lives!

Let me share another story. George Mueller owned an orphanage in England, and at breakfast one morning, the cooks told Mueller that there was no food to serve. Mueller didn't complain, worry, or become uneasy. He had the dishes, cups, and silverware placed on the tables, and everyone sat down to eat. Mueller began praying, "Thank you for what you are going to give us to eat."

GRATITUDE

When he finished praying, there was a knock at the door. The baker who was at the door said, "God told me that you didn't have food for breakfast, so I got up at two o'clock this morning and made you bread. Here," he said, unloading loaves of bread for Mueller. Then a few minutes later, there was another knock on the door. It was the milkman. "My cart broke down in front of your orphanage. Rather than let the milk spoil, I'd like to give it to the children." Their needs were provided for through another prayer of praise.

Praising God is the highest form of prayer. God wants us to praise Him even in the middle of our difficulties, the pandemic, the riots, the injustices, and the other challenges we face. When we praise God in the middle of our difficulties, we show God that we trust Him. We are also saying to ourselves that God is bigger than the challenges we face. God is a God that can open prison doors, release chains, provide food, and can part the Red Sea. The Bible is filled with many stories of the amazing things God has done. If God can do these amazing things, don't you think He can handle the big problems and difficulties we face?

My challenge to you today is that you keep a gratitude journal of things you are thankful for and that you also begin a thirty-one-day gratitude challenge. In those thirty-one days, instead of praying for your own needs, praise God and pray for others. Praise and gratitude help us focus on positive things and help us develop an attitude of positivity and hope. Even in these difficult trying times, we can learn to have an attitude of gratitude. We can praise God for the things He does for others as well as what he does for us. May we learn to praise God as Paul and Silas did in fetters in prison. May we learn to dance even in our

GRATITUDE

sorrow. May we learn to trust and have the faith of Mueller that God will provide for our daily needs.

God, please give us a heart of gratitude and thankfulness. May we be able to see beyond our circumstances. Open our eyes, Father, to the solutions you have for us. Fill our hearts and minds with thankfulness, praise, and gratitude. Amen.

← 10 →

Preventing Relapse

My grandfather was a pilot. He owned a small Cessna that he loved to fly. As a young child, I loved watching as he meticulously evaluated every one of his instruments and his entire plane prior to taking off. I loved flying with my grandfather, and I trusted him as a pilot. Over the years, this vision has stuck in my mind as I've realized that God wants to be the pilot of our life. Our job is to sit back and allow him to take over the controls of our plane. When we do, miracles and solutions happen in our life. This is what the concept of relinquishing our life to God means. It means allowing God to be the pilot of our life. This is what it means to turn our will and our life over to the care of God. We must allow him to be the pilot of our life.

It also means taking off our masks. When I went to the denominational churches I grew up in, I always felt the need to put on a mask, but I've never been a good mask wearer. My days of mask-wearing frustrated me because I knew when I went into a church that I had to pretend that I was okay. When others asked how I was, people only wanted to hear that life was good. So I responded with rote happy phrases, stuffed my pain down inside, and put on my smiling mask. I never felt like I could share about my painful life, so I'd wear my mask, sit through the service with my kids, and often leave church in tears.

PREVENTING RELAPSE

In recovery, though, we can finally take our masks off and be real. This allows us to be vulnerable and transparent with God, ourselves, and others.

Our job is to take our masks off and ask ourselves questions like:

- Are we hurting emotionally or physically?
- Are we angry about anything or anyone?
- Are there any people we need to make amends to?
- Are there any boundaries we need to work on with people?
- Are we staying connected, or are we isolating?
- Are we having our daily quiet time?
- Are we meeting our recovery goals?

Taking our masks off allows us to be real with God, ourselves, and others. This is an important part of our recovery journey because we can't heal if we don't face our feelings, thoughts, and behaviors. Taking our masks off allows God to finally work in our lives. It is also the beginning of peace. We no longer have a reason to hide. We can finally be ourselves. When we become complacent in our recovery, relapse can happen.

We have spent many hours and much time and effort working hard to climb the mountain in front of us. We are finally at the summit, looking down. We have received our victory; we have made it to the top, and we feel good. But often, when we are at the mountain's summit, we fall, we begin to lose our grip and slide down. Even during our highs, victories, and successes, we must remember to keep our triggers in mind. We must identify those things that cause us to slip so we don't begin to relapse in our recovery.

What are the things that trigger you?

PREVENTING RELAPSE

- Social media?
- Certain people?
- Places?
- Internet?
- Certain food?
- Isolation?
- Stress?
- The news?
- Negative thoughts?
- Depression, fear, or anxiety?
- Anger?

We must step out of denial and face the things that cause us to slip.

We also must develop a strategy to help us when we feel like we are slipping. This will help prevent us from relapsing.

What is the plan that you have in place?

- Picking up the phone and calling your accountability team?
- Texting your accountability team?
- Calling or texting your sponsor?
- Taking a walk or exercising?
- Listening to music?
- Journaling?
- Praying?
- Singing?
- Playing a musical instrument?
- Drawing or making other art?
- Working on a project?

PREVENTING RELAPSE

We need to identify what works for us to prevent relapse. We also need to ask God to help us. He always has an answer and solution that is right for each of us. Stay connected to God and allow Him to give you the answer that is right for you.

The last thing I want you to hold onto is this thought. When my son was little, I remember struggling to teach him how to ride a bike. He was terrified of falling, even when I held him the entire time he was on the bike. Finally, I decided to put him on his sister's smaller bike, and I used his Karate belt as a security belt. He soon learned to ride his bike. Recovery is like learning to ride a bike. We are wobbly and imperfect at first, but we finally learn what works for us, and we begin to take off.

Even if, at times when you slip and fall, your job is not to focus on falling, relapsing, and failure. Instead, focus on the following image. Imagine a child slipping and falling. The child's mother runs and scoops the child into her arms, offering comfort and help. This is what God does for us. He still loves us, comforts us, and helps us. We must not give up. God never gives up on us, so we must not give up on ourselves. Isaiah 54:10 says, "Though the mountains be shaken and the hills be removed. My unfailing love for you will not be shaken."

We may slip and fall at times, but God still loves us! His love is unconditional, with no strings attached. He wants to help us heal and succeed. Success is failure turned inside out. We may fall, but our job is to get back up and keep moving on. This is how we find success.

← 11 →

Feelings and the Arrows of Truth

So far, we have covered many topics and stories. Now I want to return to the discussions we had about our feelings. It's time now for us to identify our thoughts and feelings clearly. What emotions do you feel continuously? What emotions do you feel occasionally? What triggers these feelings? What circumstances happened in your life to cause these thoughts? Let's start to unpack this.

To help you, let me share two more Bible stories. Job is a book filled with a lot of pain. Initially, things went so well for Job. He had wealth and many children, but God allowed Satan to take it all away. Job's children died, his wealth was stolen from him, and he was covered in painful boils. His wife encouraged him to curse God and die. He refused. But he must have felt alone and isolated. Even his friends failed to encourage him. It was a very challenging time in his life. He faced grief, sorrow, pain, suffering, loneliness, rejection, isolation. Keep adding to the list of feelings he had.

But God redeemed his life. More children were born to him, and his wealth increased to more than he initially had. Now he is filled with different feelings. Jot down these feelings he might have experienced.

FEELINGS AND THE ARROWS OF TRUTH

Let's turn to one more story in the Bible, the story of Ruth. I love this book in the Bible. We read about Naomi, who left her homeland of Israel with her husband and settled in a foreign land. Pain came to Naomi when her husband and two sons died. She wanted to return to her home, but she told her daughters-in-law to stay in their homelands so they could find new husbands. But Ruth refused to stay. Instead, she insisted on coming with Naomi. She loved her mother-in-law and insisted on returning to Israel with Naomi.

Ruth went into the fields to glean, picking up sheaves of grain left behind by the field hands so she could bring food home to her mother-in-law. She ended up working in the fields of Boaz. When Boaz saw what Ruth was doing for Naomi, he admired her compassion. He told Ruth, "Do not work in anyone else's fields. Stay in mine, and I will make sure that the workers give you what you need." True to his word Ruth was provided for as she worked in his fields.

The story continues. Ruth brings home food to Naomi that she had gleaned during the day. Immediately Naomi knows that someone has been looking out for both of them. "Who's field have you been gleaning in?" Naomi asks.

"Boaz's fields."

Naomi eventually tells Ruth that Boaz is their Kinsman Redeemer, a relative that has a right to restore what is rightfully someone's to have.

During threshing time, Naomi encouraged Ruth to go down to the threshing floor where Boaz was working late at night and lay down at his feet.

Ruth obeyed her mother-in-law.

Boaz woke up late at night and realized someone was at his feet, and he sat up trying to figure out who it was.

"Who are you?" he asked.

FEELINGS AND THE ARROWS OF TRUTH

"I am your servant Ruth," she said. "Spread the corner of your garment over me since you are a kinsman-Redeemer."

Boaz blessed Ruth because she had not chased after a younger man. He promised to do what she asked. But he told her that someone nearer in kin to her was a Kinsman-Redeemer. He told her to stay for the night, but in the morning, he would talk to this man and see if he wanted to be her redeemer, and if he didn't, Boaz promised that he would be her Kinsman-Redeemer.

She lay at his feet until morning, and before anyone could be recognized, he said, "Don't let it be known that a woman came to the threshing floor."

Then he told her to put out her shawl, and he poured six measures of barley into her shawl.

And the Bible tells us that the closer Kinsman-Redeemer was unable to redeem Ruth, so Boaz became Naomi and Ruth's Kinsman-Redeemer, and Boaz married Ruth.

This story begins with feelings of sorrow, pain, anguish, loneliness, and bitterness. But it ends with hope, joy, healing, and restoration.

Now it is your turn to begin to look back over your life. Think about your mother and father, your childhood, your young adult years, and your adult years. Go back in time and list out events in your life. Think about how these things made you feel. Think about how these events impacted your life emotionally, spiritually, and physically. What habits or addictions do you struggle with? Start to identify these things in your life. And last of all, identify anyone in your life that you have hurt or anyone who has hurt you.

Now we have gotten to the step where we can begin to look at our feelings and thoughts. After all this work, we

FEELINGS AND THE ARROWS OF TRUTH

should understand where they come from and understand more about why we feel the way we do.

Next, we begin to change our minds. To renew our minds, we must begin to identify our feelings. Below I have listed some feelings. This is not an exhaustive list. Add to the list. I'm sure there are many other feelings you feel from time to time.

- Anger
- Fear
- Worthless
- Abandoned
- Isolated
- Unloved
- Unappreciated
- Depression
- Anxiety
- Overwhelmed
- Darkness
- Guilt
- Shame
- Hopelessness
- Grief

Let's attach scriptures to each of these feelings and turn them around into positive things. To do this, we need to identify the dark emotion and find its antonym. Anxiety is a dark feeling, but the opposite light feeling is calmness and serenity. Our next step is to attach a Bible text to this that teaches us a truth so we can focus on the positive feelings of calmness and serenity. This process helps us refute the attacks of Satan. When he tells us that we are worthless and nobody likes us, we can find a scripture verse to claim.

FEELINGS AND THE ARROWS OF TRUTH

Emotions can take time to identify. Some experiences lead to many emotions. When a person's mind is flooded with emotion, it may be most comfortable to stuff the feelings down inside, making it difficult to identify all emotions. When we stuff our feelings deep down inside, we stop feeling everything, including joy. Denying our feelings is also dangerous because eventually, emotions overflow and bouts of anger and rage may occur.

We must be willing to face our feelings so we can heal and have peace and serenity in our lives. To help us understand our emotions, I have color-coded them into groups. I have also paired each dark emotion with the opposite light emotion God can help us have as we begin our recovery and healing process.

Remember the story I told about my Mordor day? After this ordeal, I was reminded of Jesus in the wilderness. The story takes place in Matthew 4:1-11. Jesus had been fasting and praying for forty days. He was in the wilderness alone, hungry and vulnerable, when Satan appeared to him to tempt him. He said, "If you are the Son of God, tell these stones to become bread."

Jesus answered, "It is written: 'Man shall not live on bread alone, but on every word that comes from the mouth of God.'"

Then the devil took him to the holy city and had Him stand on the highest point of the temple. "If you are the Son of God," he said, "throw yourself down." Then Satan quoted a Bible verse from Psalm 91 that the angels would lift Him up in their hands so He would not strike His foot on a stone.

But Jesus knew the truth. The miracles were not for His own selfish desires. So He told Satan not to put the Lord to the test.

FEELINGS AND THE ARROWS OF TRUTH

Again the Devil tempted Jesus. This time it was with greed. Satan took Jesus up high in the mountains and showed Him the kingdoms of the world. "All this I will give you if you bow down and worship me." But Satan did not realize that all this already belonged to God.

But Jesus responded with, "Away from me, Satan! For it is written: 'Worship the Lord your God, and serve Him only.'"

Then the Bible says that Satan left, and angels came to minister to Jesus.

Over and over in my mind, this story replayed after the events of a few days ago. I, too, was hammered by Satan, but unlike Jesus, I didn't stop him in his tracks when his steady banter first began. I allowed him to get me down and to fill me with regret and hopelessness. But God began to speak to me. "Whose voice are you going to listen to, mine or Satan's?"

The choice is always ours. Always. We have the power to command Satan to leave. We all have that power. When we do, then God comes to minister to us, comfort us, and provide us with peace and serenity all over again. This is a daily choice of ours. Whose voice will we choose to listen to today? The voice of comfort or the voice of regret. I choose to listen to God's voice. How about you? I know He loves you and me, He cares about you and me, and He is aware of every problem we face, big or little. Best of all, He has a solution for each and every one of these challenges. He will make a way.

Now is the beginning of our action plan to refute the arrows of Satan. Join me in this process. We all can find victory over the lies of Satan. We must learn to be like Jesus. When Satan comes at us with lies, we must learn to attach scriptures to them. The only way to free our minds of lies

FEELINGS AND THE ARROWS OF TRUTH

is by filling them with truth. It is time we develop an action plan to ward off the fiery attacks of Satan.

Identify the feelings and thoughts Satan attacks you with. Your first step is to attach positive thoughts to the lies Satan has created in your mind. Then attach scriptures from the list of feelings that refute these lies with truth.

Each feeling is color-coded to help you identify its type. The light attributed to each of the feelings is highlighted in yellow identifying God's light in our life.

Use the pages in the following chapters to attach scriptures to the lies Satan presses you with.

Red = Anger, Hate, Bitterness
Orange = Anxiety and Fear
Green = Envy, Jealousy, Greed
Blue = Sadness, Grief
Purple = Low Self Worth
Pink = Coldness, Distance, Aloofness
Black = Suicidal Feelings
Grey = Exhaustion. Ever heard the phrase "Work themselves to death?"
Yellow = Happy, Light Emotions: Every emotion has a hyphen beside it that has the opposite Light Emotion.

← 12 →

Anger

Feelings are not right or wrong. All humans have feelings. However, it is essential to connect with yourself and begin the process of uncovering the reason for your emotions. How do you feel right now? Honor it. It's totally okay to feel that way. Also, be aware that some actions arising from those feelings may not be so good. My prayer for you is that you will begin to connect with yourself and begin to understand the breadth of your feelings.

Anger is an emotion that many of us face. It is often the emotion that is easiest to feel. You may stuff your emotions inside so you don't have to feel them, but this may result in blowing up and becoming angry. Eventually, all of your feelings must come out and be released. But unfortunately, the result is not so pretty.

To find peace and healing, befriend your feelings rather than stuff them inside. Every feeling has its place. Every emotion can help you somehow, and every emotion can hold you back.

Scripture shares the story of Jesus getting angry with the money changers in John 2:13-16 when they were in the temple of God, and He made them leave. Jesus had emotions and feelings too. He was angry and sad at how the people were desecrating His temple. He used His anger to remove the people who were doing what they shouldn't

ANGER

be doing in His temple. He set a boundary with the people who did not treat His temple with reverence.

Anger can be used for good. It can help you know when your boundaries are being violated and help you to realize that you need to make changes and restore your boundaries. God's help can guide you, so you don't use anger in harmful ways and injure yourself or others.

Red = Anger/Hatred/Bitterness

Anger – Calm

Proverbs 14:17 says, "People with a hot temper do foolish things; wiser people remain calm." Good News Bible. Father please help me to remain calm and not do anything foolish in my anger.

Proverbs 14:29 says, "People with understanding control their anger; a hot temper shows great foolishness." NLT Father today I am feeling so angry. Please help me control my anger through your power. Fill me with your wisdom so I don't do something hasty in my wrath. Thank you, Father, for helping me.

James 1:19-20 says, "Everyone should be quick to listen, slow to speak and slow to become angry, because human anger does not produce the righteousness that God desires." NIV

Proverbs 15:18 says, "A hot-tempered man stirs up strife, but he who is slow to anger quiets contention. ESV

ANGER

Proverbs 15:1 says, "A soft answer turns away wrath, but a harsh word stirs up anger." ESV

Bitter – Contentment, Compassionate, Admiration

Ephesians 4:31 says, "Get rid of all bitterness, rage and anger, brawling and slander, along with every form of malice. Be kind and compassionate to one another, forgiving each other, just as in Christ God forgave you." NIV

Proverbs 17:22 says, "A joyful heart is good medicine, but a crushed spirit dries up the bones." ESV

Philippians 4:11-13 says, "I have learned to be content whatever the circumstances. I know what it is to be in need, and I know what it is to have plenty. I have learned the secret of being content in any and every situation, whether well fed or hungry, whether living in plenty or in want. I can do everything through him who gives me strength." NIV

Psalm 19:14 says, "Let the words of my mouth and the meditation of my heart be acceptable in your sight, O Lord, my rock and my redeemer." ESV

Cynical – Kind

Hebrews 4:12-13 says, "For the word of God is living and active. Sharper than any double-edged sword, it penetrates even to dividing soul and spirit, joints and marrow; it judges the thoughts and attitudes of the heart. Nothing in all creation is hidden from God's sight. Everything is uncovered and laid bare

ANGER

before the eyes of Him to whom we must give account." NIV

Ephesians 4:29 says, "Let no corrupting talk come out of your mouths, but only such as is good for building up, as fits the occasion, that it may give grace to those who hear." ESV

Philippians 4:8-9 says, "Finally, brothers, whatever is true, whatever is noble, whatever is right, whatever is pure, whatever is lovely, whatever is admirable—if anything is excellent or praiseworthy —think about such things. Whatever you have learned or received or heard from me, or seen in me —put it into practice. And the God of peace will be with you." NIV

Ephesians 4:31-32 says, "Get rid of all bitterness, rage and anger, brawling and slander, along with every form of malice. Be kind and compassionate to one another, forgiving each other, just as in Christ God forgave you." NIV

Disgruntled/Dissatisfied – Content

Job 11:16-18 says, "You will forget your misery; you will remember it as waters that have passed away. And your life will be brighter than the noonday; its darkness will be like the morning. And you will feel secure, because there is hope; you will look around and take your rest in security." ESV

Psalm 40:1-3 says, "I waited patiently for the Lord; He inclined to me and heard my cry. He drew me up from the pit of destruction, out of the miry bog, and

ANGER

set my feet upon a rock, making my steps secure. He put a new song in my mouth, a song of praise to our God. Many will see and fear, and put their trust in the Lord." ESV

Philippians 4:11-13 says, "I have learned to be content whatever the circumstances. I know what it is to be in need, and I know what it is to have plenty. I have learned the secret of being content in any and every situation, whether well fed or hungry, whether living in plenty or in want. I can do everything through Him who gives me strength." NIV

Luke 6:21 says, "Blessed are you who hunger now, for you will be satisfied. Blessed are you who weep now, for you will laugh." NIV Thank you, Father, for helping me remember that you are in control.

Disturbed – Collected, Calm

Psalm 42:11 says, "Why are you downcast, O my Soul? Why so disturbed within me? Put your hope in God, for I will yet praise Him, my Savior and my God." NIV

John 14:27 says, "Peace I leave with you; my peace I give you. I do not give to you as the world gives. Do not let your hearts be troubled and do not be afraid." NIV

Psalm 55:22 says, "Cast your cares on the Lord and He will sustain you; He will never let the righteous fall." NIV

ANGER

Psalm 121:1-1 says, " I lift my eyes to the hills – where does my help come from? My help comes from the Lord, the Maker of heaven and earth." NIV

Edgy – **Unruffled**

Matthew 6:34 says, "Therefore do not worry about tomorrow, for tomorrow will worry about itself. Each day has enough trouble of its own." NIV

Exodus 14:14 says, "The Lord will fight for you; you need only to be still." NIV Thank you Father for fighting for me.

Psalm 94:19 says, "When the cares of my heart are many, your consolations cheer my soul." ESV

Psalm 55:22 says, "Cast your burden on the Lord, and He will sustain you; He will never permit the righteous to be moved." ESV

II Thessalonians 3:16 says, "Now may the Lord of peace Himself give you peace at all times and in every way. The Lord be with all of you." NIV

Exasperated – **Composed**

Psalm 107:29 says, "He stilled the storm to a whisper; the waves of the sea were hushed." NIV

John 14:27 says, "Peace I leave with you; my peace I give to you. Not as the world gives do I give to you. Let not your hearts be troubled, neither let them be afraid." ESV

Philippians 4:6 says, "Be anxious for nothing, but in everything by prayer and supplication with

ANGER

thanksgiving let your requests be made known to God." NASB

Frustrated – <mark>Relaxed</mark>

Psalm 55:22 says, "Cast your cares on the Lord and He will sustain you; He will never let the righteous fall. NIV

John 16:33 says, "I have told you these things, so that in me you may have peace. In this world you will have trouble. But take heart! I have overcome the world. NIV

Philippians 4:7 says, "And the peace of God, which surpasses all understanding, will guard your hearts and your minds in Christ Jesus." ESV

Psalm 145:18-19 says, "The Lord is near to all who call on Him, to all who call on Him in truth. He fulfills the desire of those who fear Him; He also hears their cry and saves them." ESV

Furious – <mark>Calm</mark>

Proverbs 15:1 says, "A soft answer turns away wrath, but a harsh word stirs up anger." ESV

Proverbs 14:29 says, "A patient man has great understanding, but a quick-tempered man promotes folly." BSB

Proverbs 15:18 says, "A hot-tempered man stirs up strife, but he who is slow to anger quiets contention." ESV

ANGER

James 1:19-20 says, "Know this, my beloved brothers: let every person be quick to hear, slow to speak, slow to anger; for the anger of man does not produce the righteousness of God." ESV

Psalm 34:14 says, "Turn away from evil and do good; seek peace and pursue it." ESV

Grouchy – Good Humored

I Thessalonians 5:16-18 says, "Be joyful always; pray continually; give thanks in all circumstances, for this is God's will for you in Christ Jesus." NIV

Philippians 4:4-7 says, "Rejoice in the Lord always. I will say it again: Rejoice! Let your gentleness be evident to all. The Lord is near. Do not be anxious about anything, but in everything, by prayer and petition, with thanksgiving, present your requests to God. And the peace of God, which transcends all understanding, will guard your hearts and your minds in Christ Jesus." NIV

Galatians 5:22-23 says, "But the fruit of the Spirit is love, joy, peace, patience, kindness, goodness, faithfulness, gentleness and self-control." NIV

Psalm 28:7 says, "The Lord is my strength and my shield; my heart trusts in Him, and I am helped. My heart leaps for joy and I will give thanks to Him in song." NIV

Hate/Despise – Love

Proverbs 10:12 says, "Hatred stirs up dissension, but love covers over all wrongs." NIV

ANGER

Proverbs 15:17 says, "Better a meal of vegetables where there is love than a fattened calf with hatred." NIV

I John 2:9-11 says, "Anyone who claims to be in the light but hates is brother is still in the darkness. Whoever loves his brother lives in the light, and there is nothing in him to make him stumble. But whoever hates a brother is in the darkness and walks around in the darkness; He does not know where he is going, because the darkness has blinded him." NIV

I John 4:19-20 says, "We love because He first loved us. If anyone says, "I love God," yet hates his brother, he is a liar. For anyone who does not love his brother, whom he has seen, cannot love God, whom he has not seen." NIV

Hostile – Friendly/Amiable

Proverbs 22:24 says, "Do not make friends with a hot-tempered man, do not associate with one easily angered." NIV

Colossians 3:8 says, "But now you must rid yourselves of all such things as these: anger, rage, malice, slander, and filthy language from your lips." NIV

Psalm 19:14 says, "Let the words of my mouth and the meditation of my heart be acceptable in your sight, O Lord, my rock and my redeemer." ESV

Hebrews 4:12 says, "For the word of God is living and active. Sharper than any double-edged sword, it

ANGER

penetrates even to dividing soul and spirit, joints and marrow; it judges the thoughts and attitudes of the heart. Nothing in all creation is hidden from God's sight. Everything is uncovered and laid bare before the eyes of Him to whom we must give account." NIV

Impatient – Patient

Psalm 40:1 says, "I waited patiently for the Lord; He turned to me and heard my cry." NIV

Colossians 3:12 says, "Therefore, as God's chosen people, holy and dearly loved, clothe yourselves with compassion, kindness, humility, gentleness, and patience." NIV

II Chronicles 15:7 says, "But as for you, be strong and do not give up, for your work will be rewarded." NIV

I Corinthians 2:9 says, "No eye has seen, no ear has heard, no mind has conceived what God has prepared for those who love him." NIV

Isaiah 55:8-9 says, "For my thoughts are not your thoughts, neither are your ways my ways, declares the Lord. As the heavens are higher than the earth, so are my ways higher than your ways and my thoughts than your thoughts." NIV

Irate – Pleased

Proverbs 29:11 says, "A fool gives full vent to his anger, but a wise man keeps himself under control." NIV

ANGER

Ecclesiastes 7:9 says, "Do not be quickly provoked in your spirit, for anger resides in the lap of fools." NIV

Proverbs 15:1 says, "A gentle answer turns away wrath, but a harsh word stirs up anger." NIV

Proverbs 15:18 says, "A hot-tempered man stirs up dissension, but a patient man calms a quarrel." NIV

Proverbs 14:29 says, "Whoever is slow to anger has great understanding, but he who has a hasty temper exalts folly." ESV

Proverbs 29:22 says, "A man of wrath stirs up strife, and one given to anger causes much transgression." ESV

Irritated – Relieved

Proverbs 15:1 says, "A soft answer turns away wrath, but a harsh word stirs up anger." ESV

Philippians 4:7-9 says, "And the peace of God, which surpasses understanding, will guard your hearts and minds through Christ Jesus. Finally, brethren, whatever things are true, whatever things are noble, whatever things are just, whatever things are pure, whatever things are lovely, whatever things are of good report, if there is any virtue and if there is anything praiseworthy-meditate on these things. The things which you learned and received and heard and saw in me, these do, and the God of peace will be with you." NKJV

James 1:2-4 says, "My brethren, count it all joy when you fall into various trials, knowing that the testing

ANGER

of your faith produces patience. But let patience have its perfect work, that you may be perfect and complete, lacking nothing." NKJV

James 1:19-20 says, "So then, my beloved brethren, let every man be swift to hear, slow to speak, slow to wrath; for the wrath of man does not produce the righteousness of God." NKJV

Moody – Steady/Even-Tempered/Stable

Psalm 55:22 says, "Cast your cares on the Lord and He will sustain you; He will never let the righteous fall." NIV

Philippians 4:6-7 says, "Do not be anxious about anything, but in everything, by prayer and petition, with thanksgiving, present your requests to God. And the peace of God, which transcends all understanding, will guard your hearts and minds in Christ Jesus." NIV

Isaiah 26:3 says, "You keep him in perfect peace whose mind is stayed on You, because he trusts in You." ESV

James 4:7 says, "So humble yourselves before God. Resist the devil, and he will flee from you." NLT

Rage – Self-Controlled

Proverbs 14:17 says, "People with a hot temper do foolish things; wiser people remain calm." Father, help remove my hot temper. Please help fill me with calmness that comes from me with calmness that comes from you. GNT

ANGER

Galatians 5:22-23 says, "But the fruit of the Spirit is love, joy, peace, patience, kindness, goodness, faithfulness, gentleness and self-control." NIV Father remove my anger and rage and fill me with the fruit of the spirit.

I Corinthians 10:13 says, "No temptation has seized you except what is common to man. And God is faithful; He will not let you be tempted beyond what you can bear. But when you are tempted, He will also provide a way out so that you can stand up under it." Thank you, Father, for helping to remove my rage. NIV

Proverbs 29:11 says, "A fool gives full vent to his anger, but a wise man keeps himself under control." NIV

Psalm 4:4 says, "Don't sin by letting anger control you. Think about it overnight and remain silent." NLT

Resentment – Joy

Colossians 3:12-13 says, "Put on then, as God's chosen ones, holy and beloved, compassionate hearts, kindness, humility, meekness, and patience, bearing with one another and, if one has a complaint against another, forgiving each other; as the Lord has forgiven you, so you also must forgive." ESV

Ephesians 4:31-32 says, "Get rid of all bitterness, rage, anger, harsh words, and slander, as well as all types of evil behavior. Instead, be kind to each other,

ANGER

tenderhearted, forgiving one another, just as God through Christ has forgiven you." NLT

Luke 6:37 says, "Do not judge others, and you will not be judged. Do not condemn others, or it will come back against you. Forgive others, and you will be forgiven." NLT

Romans 12:17-18 says, "Do not repay anyone evil for evil. Be careful to do what is right in the eyes of everybody. If it is possible, as far as it depends on you, live at peace with everyone." NIV

Vengeance – Forgiveness

Romans 12:21 says, "Don't let evil conquer you, but conquer evil by doing good." NLT

Matthew 5:8 says, "Blessed are the pure in heart, for they shall see God." Father help my mind to be filled with your purity, goodness, and thoughtfulness rather than vengeance. ESV

I Peter 3:9 says, "Do not repay evil with evil or insult with insult, but with blessing, because to this you were called so that you may inherit a blessing." NIV

I Thessalonians 5:15 says, "Make sure that nobody pays back wrong for wrong, but always try to be kind to each other and to everyone else." NIV

Matthew 18:21-22 says, "Then Peter came to Jesus and asked, 'Lord, how many times shall I forgive my brother when he sins against me? Up to seven times?' Jesus answered, 'I tell you, not seven times, but seventy-seven times.'" NIV

ANGER

Ephesians 4:31-32 says, "Get rid of all bitterness, rage and anger, brawling and slander, along with every form of malice. Be kind and compassionate to one another, forgiving each other, just as in Christ God forgave you." NIV

Vindictive – Merciful

Psalm 51:1-2 "Have mercy on me, O God, according to your unfailing love; according to your great compassion blot out my transgressions. Wash away all my iniquity and cleanse me from my sin." NIV

Matthew 6:14 says, "For if you forgive men when they sin against you, your heavenly Father will also forgive you." NIV

Romans 12:17, 18 says, "Do not repay anyone evil for evil. Be careful to do what is right in the eyes of everybody. If it is possible, as far as it depends on you, live at peace with everyone." NIV

I Thessalonians 5:15 says, "See that no one repays anyone evil for evil, but always seek to do good to one another and to everyone." ESV

← 13 →

Anxiety

Anxiety. Peace. These polar opposite words toyed with my mind during the pandemic as anxiety and fear continued escalating with each passing day. But I couldn't join it. I had to step away from it all. I could choose anxiety, or I could choose peace and sanity.

Anxiety can come at you from so many different angles. It can hold you in a death grip, making it difficult to function and live. The tentacles of anxiety can destroy your life if you allow them to.

Through my recovery work, I have learned to listen to the voice of God. He comforts, loves, provides hope, fills us with joy, encourages us, fills us with faith, and causes us to be courageous. May you begin the process of removing the lies that trap you in anxiety. May you choose to be filled with the truth that fills you with hope, peace, joy, and sanity.

Anxiety and fear may be firmly wrapped around your neck and mind and can be challenging, all-consuming emotions. But always remember that God is with you even when anxiety makes life difficult. May you cling to Him. May you allow God to guide you and help you.

Orange = Worry/Anxiety/Panic/Frustration/Frazzled

ANXIETY

Afraid – ==Courageous==

Joshua 1:9 says, "Be strong and courageous. Do not be terrified; do not be discouraged, for the Lord your Good will be with you wherever you go." NIV

Isaiah 41:10 says, "So do not fear, for I am with you; do not dismayed, for I am your God. I will strengthen you and help you; I will uphold you with my righteous right hand." NIV

Psalm 23:4 says, "Even though I walk through the valley of the shadow of death, I will fear no evil, for you are with me; your rod and your staff, they comfort me." NIV

Psalm 27:1 says, "The Lord is my light and my salvation—whom shall I fear? The Lord is the stronghold of my life—of whom shall I be afraid?" NIV

Deuteronomy 31:6 says, "Be strong and courageous. Do not be afraid or terrified because of them, for the Lord your God goes with you; He will never leave you nor forsake you." NIV

John 14:27 says, "Peace I leave with you; my peace I give you. I do not give to you as the world gives. Do not let your hearts be troubled and do not be afraid." NIV

Psalm 91:4-5 says, "He will cover you with His feathers, and under His wings you will find refuge; His faithfulness will be your shield and rampart. You will not fear the terror of night, nor the arrow that flies by day, nor the pestilence that stalks in the

ANXIETY

darkness, nor the plague that destroys at midday." NIV

Aggravated – ==Pacify==

Psalm 55:22 says, "Cast your cares on the Lord and He will sustain you; He will never let the righteous fall." NIV

Philippians 4:6-7 says, "Do not be anxious about anything, but in every situation, by prayer and petition, with thanksgiving, present your requests to God. And the peace of God, which surpasses all understanding, will guard your hearts and minds in Christ Jesus." NIV

John 14:27 says, "Peace is what I leave with you; it is my own peace that I give you. I do not give it as the world does. Do not be worried and upset; do not be afraid." Good News Bible

Isaiah 41:10 says, "Fear not, for I am with you; be not dismayed, for I am your God. I will strengthen you, yes, I will help you, I will uphold you with my righteous right hand." KJV

Psalm 94:19 says, "When anxiety was great within me, your consolation brought me joy." NIV

Agitated – ==Calm==

Proverbs 12:25 says, "Anxiety weighs down the heart, but a kind word cheers it up." NIV

Philippians 4:6 says, "Do not be anxious about anything, but in every situation, by prayer and

ANXIETY

petition, with thanksgiving, present your requests to God." NIV

Isaiah 41:13 says, "For I am the Lord your God who takes hold of your right hand and says to you, do not fear; I will help you." NIV

John 14:27 says, "Peace I give to you, My peace I give to you; not as the world gives do I give to you. Let not your heart be troubled, neither let it be afraid." NKJV

Anxiety – Calmness/Serenity

Psalm 23:2-3 says, "He makes me lie down in green pastures, He leads me beside quiet waters, He restores my soul." NIV

I Peter 5:7 says, "Cast all your anxiety on Him because He cares for you." NIV

Psalm 27:1 says, "The Lord is my light and my salvation – whom shall I fear? The Lord is the stronghold of my life—of whom shall I be afraid?" NIV

Apprehensive – Confident

Philippians 4:6-7 says, "Do not be anxious about anything, but in everything, by prayer and petition, with thanksgiving, present your requests to God. And the peace of God, which transcends all understanding, will guard your hearts and your minds in Christ Jesus." NIV

ANXIETY

Psalm 116:1-2 says, "I love the Lord, for He heard my voice; He heard my cry for mercy. Because He turned His ear to me, I will call on Him as long as I live." NIV

Isaiah 41:10 says, "So do not fear, for I am with you; do not be dismayed, for I am your God. I will strengthen you and help you; I will uphold you with my righteous right hand." NIV

Belligerence – Willingness

Proverbs 29:1 says, "A man who remains stiff-necked after many rebukes will suddenly be destroyed—without remedy." NIV

Proverbs 28:14 says, "Blessed is the one who always trembles before God, but whoever hardens their heart falls into trouble." NIV

Proverbs 16:18 says, "Pride goes before destruction, and a haughty spirit before a fall." NIV

Distressed – Encouraged

Psalm 32:7-8 says, "You are my hiding place; you will protect me from trouble and surround me with songs of deliverance. I will instruct you and teach you in the way you should go; I will counsel you with my loving eye on you." NIV

Psalm 145:18-19 says, "The Lord is near to all who call on Him, to all who call on Him in truth. He fulfills the desires of those who fear Him; He hears their cry and saves them." NIV

ANXIETY

Deuteronomy 31:6 says, "Be strong and courageous. Do not be afraid or terrified because of them, for the Lord your God goes with you; He will never leave you nor forsake you." NIV

Proverbs 12:25 says, "When you're in a tough time, it can be hard to see beyond that. But you should try to focus on the positive things around you, to help you see that your troubles are not all-consuming." Good News Bible

Psalm 34:17 says, "When the righteous cry for help, the Lord hears and delivers them out of all their troubles." NIV

Edgy – ==Relaxed==

Lamentations 3:22-23 says, "The steadfast love of the Lord never ceases; His mercies never come to an end; they are new every morning; great is your faithfulness." ESV

I Peter 5:7 says, "Cast all your anxiety on Him because He cares for you." NIV

John 14:27 says, "Peace I leave with you; my peace I give to you. Not as the world gives do I give to you. Let not your hearts be troubled, neither let them be afraid." ESV

Psalm 121:1-2 says, "I lift up my eyes to the hills – where does my help come from? My help comes from the Lord, the Maker of heaven and earth." NIV

ANXIETY

Exasperated – Pacified

Philippians 4:13 says, "I can do all things through Christ who strengthens me." NKJV

Isaiah 26:3 says, "You keep him in perfect peace whose mind is stayed on you, because He trusts in you." ESV

Isaiah 41:13 says, "For I am the Lord your God who takes hold of your right hand and says to you, do not fear; I will help you." NIV

Matthew 11:28-30 says, "Come to me, all who labor and are heavy laden, and I will give you rest. Take my yoke upon you, and learn from me, for I am gentle and lowly in heart, and you will find rest for your souls. For my yoke is easy, and my burden in light." ESV

John 14:27 says, "Peace I leave with you; my peace I give to you. Not as the world gives do I give to you. Let not your hearts be troubled, neither let them be afraid." ESV

Fear – Boldness

Isaiah 41:10 says, "So do not fear, for I am with you; do not be dismayed, for I am your God. I will strengthen you and help you; I will uphold you with my righteous right hand." NIV

Deuteronomy 31:6 says, "Be strong and courageous. Do not be afraid or terrified because of them, for the Lord your God goes with you; He will never leave you nor forsake you." NIV

ANXIETY

Psalm 46:1-3 says, "God is our refuge and strength, an ever-present help in trouble. Therefore we will not fear, though the earth gives way and the mountains fall into the heart of the sea, though its waters roar and foam and the mountains quake with their surging." NIV

Psalm 23:4 ways, "Even though I walk through the valley of the shadow of death, I will fear no evil, for you are with me; your rod and your staff, they comfort me." NIV

Psalm 34:7 says, "The angel of the Lord encamps around those who fear Him, and He delivers them." NIV

Frazzled/Frustrated – Encouraged

John 16:24 says, "Ask and you will receive, and your joy will be complete." NIV

I Peter 5:7 says, "Casting all your anxiety on Him because He cares for you." NIV

Proverbs 3:5-6 says, "Trust in the Lord with all your heart, and lean not on your own understanding; in all your ways acknowledge Him, and He shall direct your paths." NKJV

Philippians 4:8 says, "Whatever is true, whatever is noble, whatever is right, whatever is pure, whatever is lovely, whatever is admirable–if anything is excellent or praiseworthy – think about such things." NIV

ANXIETY

Frightened – ==Reassured==

Psalm 23:4 says, "Even though I walk through the valley of the shadow of death, I will fear no evil, for you are with me." NIV

Isaiah 43:1-2 says, "Fear not, for I have redeemed you; I have called you by your name; you are Mine. When you pass through the waters, I will be with you; and through the rivers, they shall not overflow you. When you walk through the fire, you shall not be burned, nor shall the flame scorch you." NKJV

Romans 8:31 says, "If God is for us, who can be against us?" NIV

Philippians 4:6-7 says, "Do not be anxious about anything, but in everything, by prayer and petition, with thanksgiving, present your requests to God. And the peace of God, which transcends all understanding, will guard your hearts and minds in Christ Jesus." NIV

Hypervigilant/Skeptical – ==Peaceful/Trusting==

Hebrews 13:6 says, "The Lord is my helper; I will not fear. What can man do to me?" NKJV

Isaiah 41:10 says, "Fear not, for I am with you; be not dismayed, for I am your God. I will strengthen you, yes, I will help you, I will uphold you with My righteous right hand." NKJV

I Peter 5:7 says, "Casting all your anxiety on Him, because He cares for you." NIV

ANXIETY

Nervous – Relaxed/Composed

Deuteronomy 31:8 says, "The Lord Himself goes before you and will be with you; He will never leave you nor forsake you. Do not be afraid; do not be discouraged." NIV

Psalm 9:9 says, "The Lord is a refuge for the oppressed, a stronghold in times of trouble." NIV

Psalm 40:1-2 says, "I waited patiently for the Lord; he turned to me and heard my cry. He lifted me out of the slimy pit, out of the mud and mire; he set my feet on a rock and gave me a firm place to stand." NIV

Isaiah 41:10 says, "Fear not, for I am with you; be not dismayed, for I am your God. I will strengthen you, Yes, I will help you, I will uphold you with My righteous right hand." NIV

Panic – Calm

Proverbs 3:26 says, "No need to panic over alarms or surprises, or predictions that doomsday's just around the corner, because God will be right there with you; He'll keep you safe and sound." Message

Deuteronomy 31:8 says, "The Lord Himself goes before you and will be with you; He will never leave you nor forsake you. Do not be afraid; do not be discouraged. NIV

Psalm 34:17 says, "The righteous cry out, and the Lord hears, and delivers them out of all their troubles." NKJV

ANXIETY

Scared/Terrified/Reluctant – ==Reassured/Courageous==

Psalm 23:4 says, "Even though I walk through the valley of the shadow of death, I will fear no evil for you are with me; your rod and staff, they comfort me." NIV

Psalm 27:1 says, "The Lord is my light and my salvation—whom shall I fear? The Lord is the stronghold of my life—of whom shall I be afraid? NIV

John 14:27 says, "Peace I leave with you, My peace I give to you; not as the world gives do I give to you. Let not your hearts be troubled, neither let it be afraid." NKJV

Joshua 1:9 says, "Be strong and courageous. Do not be terrified; do not be discouraged, for the Lord your God will be with you wherever you go." NIV

Shy/Timid – ==Outgoing/Brave==

II Timothy 1:7 says, "For God did not give us a spirit of timidity, but a spirit of power, of love and of self-discipline." NIV

Deuteronomy 31:6 says, "Be strong and courageous. Do not be afraid or terrified because of them, for the Lord your God goes with you; He will never leave you nor forsake you." NIV

Worry/Uneasy – ==Peaceful/Tranquil==

Psalm 46:1 says, "God is our refuge and strength, an ever-present help in trouble." NIV

ANXIETY

Psalm 27:12 says, "The Lord is my light and my salvation; whom shall I fear? The Lord is the strength of my life; of whom shall I be afraid?" NKJV

… 14 …

Generosity

When you become focused on others and what they have, and you forget to be thankful for the things you have, you can become greedy. I see greed through the eyes of the dragon who never has enough gems, treasures, and money. His dragon's lair is his focus of attention, and he doesn't want anyone to touch it. He spends his life not being satisfied with what he has. He is constantly trying to get more and more material possessions.

Greed, in my mind, is a heart issue. God has to help us. It starts with becoming thankful for all the things that you have. It is crucial to practice gratitude journaling and keep a list of the things you are thankful for. This helps you remember all the extraordinary things you have and keeps you focused on the truth. All of us have many things to be thankful for.

Another step in removing greed from your heart is through generosity toward others. Do this by tithing to God, and do this by giving to others. Father, may you help me not have green eyes of greed but have loving, kind, and thoughtful eyes that are thankful and grateful for what I have. May I become generous, kind, and thoughtful toward others.

Green = Envy/Greed/Pride/Covetous/Lust/Selfish

GENEROSITY

Covetous – **Generous**

James 4:1-2 says, "What causes quarrels and what causes fights among you? Is it not this, that your passions are at war within you? You desire and do not have, so you murder. You covet and cannot obtain, so you fight and quarrel. You do not have, because you do not ask." ESV

I Corinthians 10:24 says, "Let no one seek his own good, but the good of his neighbor." ESV

I John 3:17 says, "If anyone has material possessions and sees his brother in need but has no pity on him, how can the love of God be in him?" NIV

Envy/Jealousy – **Appeased/Satisfied**

I Corinthians 13:4-5 says, "Love is patient, love is kind. It does not envy, it does not boast, it is not proud. It is not rude, it is not self-seeking, it is not easily angered, it keeps no record of wrongs." NIV

Philippians 2:3, 4 says, "Do nothing out of selfish ambition or vain conceit, but in humility consider others better than yourselves. Each of you should look not only to your own interests, but also to the interests of others." NIV

Philippians 2:21 says, "For everyone looks out for his own interests, not those of Jesus Christ." NIV

Greed – **Generous**

I Corinthians 10:24 says, "Let no one seek his own good, but the good of his neighbor." ESV

GENEROSITY

Proverbs 28:27 says, "He who gives to the poor will lack nothing, but he who closes his eyes to them receives many curses." NIV

Philippians 2:3-4 says, "Do nothing out of selfish ambition or vain conceit, but in humility consider others better than yourselves. Each of you should look not only to your own interests, but also to the interests of others." NIV

Lust – **Chastity/Purity**

Philippians 4:8-9 says, "Finally, brothers, whatever is true, whatever is noble, whatever is right, whatever is pure, whatever is lovely, whatever is admirable— if anything is excellent or praiseworthy—think about such things. Whatever you have learned or received or heard from me, or seen in me—put it into practice. And the God of peace will be with you." NIV

Proverbs 6:25 says, "Do not lust in your heart after her (or his) beauty or let her (or him) captivate you with her (or his) eyes." NIV

Colossians 3:5 says, "Put to death, therefore, whatever belongs to your earthly nature: sexual immorality, impurity, lust, evil desires and greed, which is idolatry." NIV

Malice – **Kindness**

Galatians 5:22-23 says, "But the fruit of the Spirit is love, joy, peace, patience, kindness, goodness, faithfulness, gentleness and self-control. NIV

GENEROSITY

John 15:13, "Greater love has no one than this, that someone lay down his life for his friends." ESV

I Corinthians 13:4-5 says, "Love is patient and kind; love does not envy or boast; it is not arrogant or rude. It does not insist on its own way; it is not irritable or resentful." ESV

Colossians 3:12-14 says, "Clothe yourselves with compassion, kindness, humility, gentleness and patience. Bear with each other and forgive whatever grievances you may have against one another. Forgive as the Lord forgave you. And over all these virtues put on love, which binds them all together in perfect unity." NIV

Pride – **Humble**

Philippians 2:5-8 says, "Your attitude should be the same as that of Christ Jesus: Who, being in very nature God, did not consider equality with God something to be grasped, but made himself nothing, taking the very nature of a servant, being made in human likeness. And being found in appearance as a man, he humbled himself and became obedient to death—even death on a cross!" NIV

James 4:10 says, "Humble yourselves before the Lord, and He will lift you up." NIV

Micah 6:8 says, "He has shown you, O man, what is good. And what does the Lord require of you? To act justly and to love mercy and to walk humbly with your God." NIV

GENEROSITY

II Chronicles 7:14 says, "If my people, who are called by my name, will humble themselves and pray and seek my face and turn from their wicked ways, then will I hear from heaven and will forgive their sin and will heal their land." NIV

Matthew 23:11-12 says, "The greatest among you will be your servant. For whoever exalts himself will be humbled, and whoever humbles himself will be exalted." NIV

I Peter 5:5 says, "God opposes the proud but gives grace to the humble." NIV

Selfish – Caring/Benevolent/Compassionate

Philippians 2:4 says, "Each of you should look not only to your own interests, but also to the interests of others." NIV

I Corinthians 10:24 says, "Nobody should seek his own good, but the good of others." NIV

Philippians 2:3-4 says, "Do nothing out of selfish ambition or vain conceit, but in humility consider others better than yourselves. Each of you should look not only to your own interests, but also to the interests of others." NIV

Galatians 6:2 says, "Carry each other's burdens, and in this way you will fulfill law of Christ." NIV

GENEROSITY

Stingy – **Charitable**

I John 3:17 says, "If anyone has material possessions and sees his brother in need but has no pity on him, how can the love of God be in him?" NIV

Proverbs 11:24 says, "One man gives freely, yet gains even more; another withholds unduly, but comes to poverty." NIV

Proverbs 28:22 says, "A stingy man is eager get rich and is unaware that poverty awaits him." NIV

Proverbs 28:27 says, "He who gives to the poor will lack nothing." NIV

II Corinthians 9:6-7 says, "Whoever sows sparingly will also reap sparingly, and whoever sows generously will also reap generously. Each man should give what he has decided in his heart to give, not reluctantly or under compulsion, for God loves a cheerful giver." NIV

Hebrews 13:5 says, "Keep your lives free from the love of money and be content with what you have." NIV

← 15 →

Sadness

For the past few months, I have been training to become a grief coach. My own journey through grief and sorrow led me down this path. I ached to become a beacon of light and hope to others facing grief and sadness. I know that this journey can be a lonely one. For so many years in my own grief, I traveled alone.

Healing from grief doesn't happen easily when you try to do it on your own. My journey was a long and difficult one. But God eventually stepped in and carried me to a grief recovery group. I walked into the group not knowing anyone, and I walked away feeling like I had known the people in the group forever. We connected deeply about our pain and grief, and I walked away from that group feeling blessed.

David Kessler talks about the journey through grief being like traveling down a river. You have to allow grief to carry you to healing. It is a process, and the journey is different for everyone. There is no magic time frame for healing from grief. I have learned that it is something that I have to live with, just like I wear a garment. I wear a robe of grief that gets thinner with time, but it has become part of who I am. It has changed me, but it has also allowed me to find meaning in my life that I never dreamed possible. That journey has taught me that God has a ministry that He is preparing me for. It took my journey through all the trials, pain, and difficulty for me to finally be prepared for this path God is opening up for me.

SADNESS

God also recently showed me that for many years I chose to disown happiness. This meant that instead of choosing happiness, I could only see sadness. But in that sadness, I learned to write and to be in touch with my feelings. My ability to find happiness happened when a friend helped me realize that I could indeed laugh again. I could find joy, but it took his presence in my life to show me that it was possible.

You can push away any feeling in your life. The choice is yours, though, to reclaim these feelings. God aches to bring wholeness and healing into your life. May God help you find this wholeness again.

Sadness and pain happen in this life. You have a choice to allow the pain to destroy and create bitterness in you, or you can learn to use it to create meaning in your life. My hope and prayer for you is that you will use the sadness, pain, heartache, and difficulties that you face for good. May God help this pain in your life to be turned into a positive blessing for others. Only God has the power to do this in your life.

Blue = Sad/Depression/Grief/Lonely

Anguish – Gladness

> II Corinthians 4:16 -18 says, "Therefore we do not lose heart. Though outwardly we are wasting away, yet inwardly we are being renewed day by day. For our light and momentary troubles are achieving for us an eternal glory that far outweighs them all. So we fix our eyes not on what is seen, but on what is unseen. For what is seen is temporary, but what is unseen is eternal." NIV

SADNESS

Matthew 11:28 says, "Come to me, all you who are weary and burdened, and I will give you rest." NIV

John 14:27 says, "Peace I leave with you; my peace I give you. I do not give to you as the world gives. Do not let your hearts be troubled and do not be afraid." NIV

Critical – Positive

Psalm 19:14 says, "Let the words of my mouth and the meditation of my heart be acceptable in your sight, O Lord, my rock and my redeemer." ESV

Proverbs 21:19 says, "It is better to live in a desert land than with a quarrelsome and fretful woman." ESV

Depressed – Joyful

Psalm 43:5 says, "Why are you downcast, O my soul? Why so disturbed within me? Put your hope in God, for I will yet praise Him, my Savior and my God." NIV

Proverbs 17:22 says, "A cheerful heart is good medicine, but a crushed spirit dries up the bones." NIV

Discouraged – Encouraged

Isaiah 42:16 says, "And I will lead the blind in a way that they do not know, in paths that they have not known I will guide them. I will turn the darkness before them into light, the rough places into level

SADNESS

ground. These are the things I do, and I do not forsake them." ESV

II Corinthians 5:7 says, "For we walk by faith, not by sight." ESV

Disgruntled – Contented

II Corinthians 12:9-10 says, "My grace is sufficient for you, for my power is made perfect in weakness. Therefore I will boast all the more gladly about my weaknesses, so that Christ's power may rest on me. That is why, for Christ's sake, I delight in weaknesses, in insults, in hardships, in persecutions, in difficulties. For when I am weak, then I am strong." NIV

Proverbs 19:23 says, "The fear of the Lord leads to life; then one rests content, untouched by trouble." NIV

Dissatisfied – Satisfied

Psalm 107:9 says, "For He satisfies the longing soul, and the hungry soul He fills with good things." ESV

Isaiah 58:11 says, "The Lord will guide you always; He will satisfy your needs in a sun-scorched land and will strengthen your frame. You will be like a well-watered garden, like a spring whose waters never fail." NIV

Gloomy – Happy

Isaiah 35:10 says, "And the ransomed of the Lord will return. They will enter Zion with singing;

SADNESS

everlasting joy will crown their heads. Gladness and joy will overtake them, and sorrow and sighing will flee away." NIV

Proverbs 17:22 says, "A cheerful heart is good medicine, but a crushed spirit dries up the bones." NIV

II Samuel 22:29 says, "You are my lamp, O Lord; the Lord turns my darkness into light." NIV

Grief – Comforted

Psalm 34:18 says, "The Lord is close to the brokenhearted and saves those who are crushed in spirit." NIV

Psalm 147:3 says, "He heals the brokenhearted and binds up their wounds." NIV

Revelation 21:4 says, "He will wipe every tear from their eyes. There will be no more death or mourning or crying or pain, for the old order of things has passed away." NIV

Matthew 5:4 says, "Blessed are those who mourn, for they will be comforted." NIV

Heartbroken – Encouraged

II Corinthians 1:3-4 says, "Blessed be the God and Father of our Lord Jesus Christ, the Father of mercies and God of all comfort, who comforts us in all our affliction, so that we may be able to comfort those who are in any affliction, with the comfort with which we ourselves are comforted by God." ESV

SADNESS

Psalm 34:18 says, "The Lord is close to the brokenhearted and saves those who are crushed in spirit." NIV

Hopeless – **Hope**

Romans 15:13 says, "May the God of hope fill you with all joy and peace as you trust in Him, so that you may overflow with hope by the power of the Holy Spirit." NIV

Jeremiah 29:11 says, "'For I know the plans I have for you,' declares the Lord, 'plans to prosper you and not to harm you, plans to give you hope and a future.'" NIV

Isaiah 40:31 says, "But those who hope in the Lord will renew their strength. They will soar on wings like eagles; they will run and not grow weary, they will walk and not be faint." NIV

Judgmental – **Positive**

Proverbs 12:25 says, "Anxiety in a man's heart weighs him down, but a good word makes him glad." ESV

Philippians 4:8 says, "Finally, brothers, whatever is true, whatever is honorable, whatever is just, whatever is pure, whatever is lovely, whatever is commendable, if there is any excellence, if there is anything worthy of praise, think about these things." ESV

SADNESS

Proverbs 10:20 says, "The tongue of the righteous is choice silver, but the heart of the wicked is of little value." NIV

I Corinthians 13:1-8, 13 says, "If I speak in the tongues of men and of angels, but have not love, I am a noisy gong or a clanging cymbal. And if I have prophetic powers, and understand all mysteries and knowledge, and if I have all faith, so as to remove mountains, but have not love, I am nothing. If I give away all I have, and if I deliver up my body to be burned, but have not love, I gain nothing. Love is patient and kind; love does not envy or boast; it is not arrogant or rude. It does not insist on its own way; it is not irritable or resentful; it does not rejoice at wrongdoing, but rejoices with the truth. Love bears all things, believes all things, hopes all things, endures all things. Love never ends . . . So now faith, hope, and love abide, these three; but the greatest of these is love." ESV

Lonely – **Befriended**

Deuteronomy 31:6 says, "Be strong and courageous. Do not be afraid or terrified because of them, for the Lord your God goes with you; He will never leave you nor forsake you." NIV

Psalm 27:10 says, "Though my father and mother forsake me, the Lord will receive me." NIV

Psalm 68:5, 6 says, "A father to the fatherless, a defender of widows, is God in His holy dwelling. God sets the lonely in families." NIV

SADNESS

Melancholy – Elated

Proverbs 17:22 says, "A cheerful heart is good medicine, but a crushed spirit dries up the bones." NIV

Psalm 40:1-2 says, "I waited patiently for the Lord; He inclined to me and heard my cry. He drew me up from the pit of destruction, out of the miry bog, and set my feet upon a rock, making my steps secure." ESV

Isaiah 41:10 says, "Fear not, for I am with you; be not dismayed; for I am your God; I will strengthen you, I will help you, I will uphold you with my righteous right hand." ESV

Negative – Positive

Ephesians 4:29 says, "Do not let any unwholesome talk come out of your mouths, but only what is helpful for building others up according to their needs, that it may benefit those who listen." NIV

Proverbs 10:20 says, "The tongue of the righteous is choice silver, but the heart of the wicked is of little value." NIV

Psalm 19:14 says, "Let the words of my mouth and the meditation of my heart be acceptable in your sight, O Lord, my rock and my redeemer." ESV

Remorse – Shamelessness

Psalm 147:3 says, "He heals the brokenhearted and binds up their wounds." NIV

SADNESS

Psalm 51:10 says, "Create in me a clean heart O God, and renew a right spirit in me." ESV

I John 1:9 says, "If we confess our sins, He is faithful and just to forgive us our sins to cleanse us from all unrighteousness." ESV

Psalm 103:12 says, "As far as the east is from the west, so far does he remove our transgressions from us." ESV

Isaiah 1:18 says, "Come now, let us reason together, says the Lord: though your sins are like scarlet, they shall be as white as snow; though they are red like crimson, they shall become like wool." ESV

Sorrow – **Happiness**

Matthew 5:4 says, "Blessed are those who mourn, for they shall be comforted." NIV

Isaiah 53:4, 5 says, "He took up our infirmities and carried our sorrows, yet we considered Him stricken by God, smitten by Him, and afflicted. But He was pierced for our transgressions, He was crushed for our iniquities; the punishment that brought us peace was upon Him, and by His wounds we are healed." NIV

Revelation 21:4 says, "He will wipe every tear from their eyes. There will be no more death or mourning or crying or pain, for the old order of things has passed away." NIV

SADNESS

Psalm 34:18 says, "The Lord is close to the brokenhearted and saves those who are crushed in spirit." NIV

Psalm 147:3 says, "He heals the brokenhearted and binds up their wounds." NIV

Teary – **Cheerful**

Psalm 30:5 says, "Weeping may remain for a night, but rejoicing comes in the morning." NIV

Psalm 30:11 says, "You turned my wailing into dancing, you removed my sackcloth and clothed me with joy." NIV

Psalm 56:8 says, "You keep track of all our sorrows. You have collected all my tears in your bottle." NLT The Message Bible says, "You've kept track of my every toss and turn through the sleepless nights, each tear entered in your ledger, each ache written in your book."

← 16 →

Children of God

Maybe your life has been a challenging one. Maybe you have faced abandonment by your family. Maybe you have felt abandoned by a church or by the people around you. Maybe you have faced abuse and rejection. Maybe you were criticized and humiliated, so you feel unworthy. Maybe your family of origin was dysfunctional. Maybe you felt isolated and alone in your family. Only you and God know your story and your pain.

Your past can lead you to stories that you tell yourself. These stories may or may not be true. Tease out the truth in your stories. You may feel worthless, struggle with low self-esteem, feel insecure, feel rejected, or abandoned, but it is time for you to reclaim the truth. It is time to focus on God's love and how He created you. He loves you enough that He died on a cross to save you. This means that you are worthy. You are a child of God; you are a child of the King. We are all princes and princesses of the King.

Purple represents royalty. You are royal. You are a child of the King, God. Knowing this helps you focus on your worth in Christ.

Purple = Ashamed/Embarrassed/Belittled/Low Self Worth/Not Good Enough/ Victimization Feelings/ Insecurity/Self-Doubt

Abandoned/Desolate – Accompanied

CHILDREN OF GOD

Isaiah 49:15-16 says, "Can a mother forget the baby at her breast and have no compassion on the child she has borne? Though she may forget, I will not forget you! See, I have engraved you on the palms of my hands; your walls are ever before me." NIV

Psalm 27:10 says, "My father and mother walked out and left me, but God took me in." Message Bible The NIV says, "Though my father and mother forsake me, the Lord will receive me."

Romans 8:37-39 says, "In all these things we are more than conquerors through Him who loved us. For I am convinced that neither death nor life, neither angels nor demons, neither the present nor the future, nor any powers, neither height nor depth, nor anything else in all creation, will be able to separate us from the love of God in Christ Jesus our Lord." NIV

Ashamed – Shameless

John 8:10-11 says, "Where are your accusers? Didn't even one of them condemn you?' 'No, Lord,' she said. And Jesus said, 'Neither do I. Go and sin no more.'" NLT

Matthew 6:14 says, "For if you forgive other people when they sin against you, your heavenly Father will also forgive you." NIV

Colossians 3:13 says, "Bear with each other and forgive one another if any of you has a grievance against someone. Forgive as the lord forgave you." NIV

CHILDREN OF GOD

Psalm 103:12 says, "As far as the eat is from the west, so far has he removed our transgressions from us." NIV

Isaiah 43:25 says, "I, even I, am He who blots out your transgressions, for my own sake, and remembers your sins no more." NIV

Brokenness – Restored

I Peter 5:10 says, "And the God of all grace, who called you to His eternal glory in Christ, after you have suffered a little while, will Himself restore you and make you strong, firm and steadfast." NIV

Psalm 34:18 says, "The Lord is close to the brokenhearted and saves those who are crushed in spirit." NIV

Psalm 147:3 says, "He heals the brokenhearted and binds up their wounds." NIV

Condemned – Forgiven

I Corinthians 2:9 says, "No eye has seen, nor ear heard, nor the heart of man imagined, what God has prepared for those who love Him." ESV

Romans 12:10 says, "Love one another with brotherly affection. Outdo one another in showing honor." ESV

Romans 5:8 says, "But God shows His love for us in that while we were still sinners, Christ died for us." ESV

CHILDREN OF GOD

John 3:16-17 says, "For God so loved the world, that He gave His only Son, that whoever believes in Him should not perish but have eternal life. For God did not send His Son into the world to condemn the world, but in order that the world might be saved through Him." ESV

Humiliated – Honor

I Corinthians 4:5 says, "He will bring to light what is hidden in darkness and will expose the motives of men's hearts." BSB

Micah 7:19 says, "You will again have compassion on us; You will tread our sins underfoot and hurl all our iniquities into the depths of the sea." NIV

Romans 8:1 "There is no condemnation now for those who live in union with Christ Jesus." GNBDC

Incapable/Helpless – Capable

I Corinthians 10:13 says, "No trial has overtaken you that is not faced by others. And God is faithful: He will not let you be tried beyond what you are able to bear, but with the trial will also provide a way out so that you may be able to endure it." NET

Philippians 4:13 says, "I can do all things through Him who strengthens me." ESV

Philippians 4:19 says, "And my God will supply every need of yours according to His riches in glory in Christ Jesus." ESV

CHILDREN OF GOD

Hebrews 13:6 says, "So we can confidently say, 'the Lord is my helper; I will not fear; what can man do to me?'" ESV

Isolated/Alone – **Included/Accompanied/ United/ Connected**

Ecclesiastes 4:9-10, 12 says, "Two people are better off than one, for they can help each other succeed. If one person falls, the other can reach out and help. But someone who falls alone is in real trouble . . . A person standing alone can be attacked and defeated, but two can stand back-to-back and conquer. Three are even better, for a triple-braided cord is not easily broken." NLT

Deuteronomy 31:8 says, "It is the Lord who goes before you; He will be with you. He will not fail you or abandon you. Do not fear or be dismayed." AMP

Isaiah 49:15-16 says, "Can a mother forget the baby at her breast and have no compassion on the child she has borne? Though she may forget, I will not forget you! See, I have engraved you on the palms of my hands; your walls are ever before me." NIV

Neglected/Overlooked – **Redeemed/Treasured**

John 10:11 says, "I am the good shepherd. The good shepherd lays down his life for the sheep." NIV

Jeremiah 31:3 says, "I have loved you with an everlasting love; I have drawn you with loving-kindness." NIV

CHILDREN OF GOD

Isaiah 43:2 says, "When you pass through the waters, I will be with you; and when you pass through the rivers, they will not sweep over you. When you walk through the fire, you will not be burned; the flames will not set you ablaze." NIV

Regret – Shamelessness

I John 1:9 says, "If we confess our sins, He is faithful and just and will forgive us our sins and purify us from all unrighteousness." NIV

Luke 15:7 says, "I tell you in the same way there will be more rejoicing in heaven over one sinner who repents than over ninety-nine righteous persons who do not need to repent." NIV

Psalm 103:12 says, "As far as the east is from the west, so far has he removed our transgressions from us." NIV

Isaiah 43:18-19 says, "Forget the former things; do not dwell on the past. See, I am doing a new thing! Now it springs up; do you not perceive it? I am making a way in the desert and streams in the wasteland." NIV

Rejected – Accepted

Romans 5:8 says, "But God shows His love for us in that while we were yet sinners Christ died for us." RSV

John 3:16 says, "For God so loved the world, that He gave His only Son, that whoever believes in Him should not perish but have eternal life." ESV

CHILDREN OF GOD

Psalm 34:18 says, "The Lord is close to the brokenhearted; He rescues those whose spirits are crushed." NLT

Psalm 27:10 says, "Though my father and mother forsake me, the Lord will receive me." NIV

I Samuel 12:22 says, "For the sake of His great name the Lord will not reject His people, because the Lord was pleased to make you His own." NIV

Self-Conscious – Confident

Ephesians 2:10 says, "For we are God's masterpiece. He has created us anew in Christ Jesus, so we can do the good things He planned for us long ago." NLT

Philippians 4:13 says, "I can do all things through Him who strengthens me." ESV

Shame – Self Confidence

Isaiah 61:7 says, "Instead of their shame my people will receive a double portion, and instead of disgrace they will rejoice in their inheritance; and so they will inherit a double portion in their land, and everlasting joy will be theirs." NIV

Jeremiah 31:3 says, "GOD told them, "I've never quit loving you and never will.

Expect love, love, and more love!" Message Bible

Romans 8:38-39 says, "For I am convinced that neither death nor life, neither angels nor demons, neither the present nor the future, nor any powers, neither height nor depth, nor anything else in all creation, will be able to separate us from the love of God that is in Christ Jesus our Lord." NIV

Isaiah 54:10 says, "Though the mountains be shaken and the hills be removed, yet my unfailing love for you _____ (insert your name) will not be shaken nor my covenant of peace be removed, says the Lord, who has compassion on you." NIV

Trapped – <mark>Freed</mark>

I Corinthians 10:13 says, "No test or temptation that comes your way is beyond the course of what others have had to face. All you need to remember is that God will never let you down; He'll never let you be pushed past your limit; He'll always be there to help you come through it." Message Bible

Romans 12:12 says, " Be joyful in hope, patient in affliction, faithful in prayer." NIV

Romans 8:31 says, "What, then, shall we say in response to these things? If God is for us, who can be against us?" NIV

Isaiah 41:10 says, "Fear not, for I am with you; be not dismayed, for I am your God, I will strengthen you, I will help you, I will uphold you with my righteous right hand." ESV

Matthew 19:26 says, "With man this is impossible, but with God all things are possible." NIV

Unloved – <mark>Cherished</mark>

CHILDREN OF GOD

Romans 5:8 says, "But God demonstrates His own love for us in this: While we were still sinners, Christ died for us." NIV

John 3:16 says, "For God so loved the world that He gave His one and only Son, that whoever believes in Him shall not perish but have eternal life." NIV

I John 4:9-12 says, "This is how God showed His love for us: God sent His only Son into the world so we might live through Him. This is the kind of love we are talking about—not that we once upon a time loved God, but that He loved us and sent His Son as a sacrifice to clear away our sins and the damage they've done to our relationship with God. My dear, dear friends, if God loved us like this, we certainly ought to love each other. No one has seen God, ever. But if we love one another, God dwells deeply within us, and His love becomes complete in us—perfect love!" Message Bible

Weak – Strong

Matthew 11:28-30 says, "Come to me, all who are weary and burdened, and I will give you rest. Take my yoke upon you and learn from me, for I am gentle and humble in heart, and you will find rest for your souls. For my yoke is easy and my burden is light." NIV

Isaiah 40:31 says, "But those who hope in the Lord will renew their strength. They will soar on wings like eagles; they will run and not grow weary, they will walk and not be faint." NIV

CHILDREN OF GOD

Psalm 23 says, "The Lord is my shepherd, I shall not be in want. He makes me lie down in green pastures, He leads me beside quiet waters, He restores my soul. He guides me in paths of righteousness for His name's sake. Even though I walk through the valley of the shadow of death, I will fear no evil, for you are with me; your rod and your staff they comfort me. You prepare a table before me in the presence of my enemies. You anoint my head with oil; my cup overflows. Surely goodness and love will follow me all the days of my life, and I will dwell in the house of the Lord forever. NIV

Worthless/Belittled/Despised – Valued

Psalm 139:13-14 says, "For you created my inmost being; you knit me together in my mother's womb. I praise you because I am fearfully and wonderfully made." NIV

Psalm 139:15, 16 says, "My frame was not hidden from you when I was made in the secret place. When I was woven together in the depths of the earth, your eyes saw my unformed body. All the days ordained for me were written in your book before one of them came to be." NIV

Isaiah 49:16 says, "I will not forget you! See, I have engraved you on the palms of my hands; your walls are ever before me." NIV

Victimized – Nurtured/Protected

Psalm 34:17-18 says, "The righteous cry out, and the Lord hears them; He delivers them from all their

CHILDREN OF GOD

troubles. The Lord is close to the brokenhearted and saves those who are crushed in spirit." NIV

II Peter 2:9 says, "The Lord knows how to rescue godly men from trials . . ." NIV

Psalm 147:3 says, "He heals the brokenhearted and binds up their wounds." NIV

← 17 →

Distance

Have you ever known a distant, cold person? Have you ever known people who are aloof? Have you ever known people who push away feelings? Distance and coldness can happen to people. Maybe it results from pain and suffering people have experienced in their lives. Maybe it's because people stuff their feelings inside and don't want to face them. Whatever the case, it can happen.

This coldness and distance can be a result of disowned feelings. When you push away your feelings, you may end up not feeling anything. You can't feel happiness or joy; you become numb, almost like a block of ice.

To become free and whole and melt that block of ice surrounding your heart, you must embrace your emotions. How are you really feeling? Are you angry about someone or something? Are you sad about an experience that happened in your life? Are you grieving over something? Do the hard but vital work of teasing out what is inside of you. Don't destroy yourself by bottling up your feelings, trapping them deep inside. Denying your feelings will only eat away at you.

Just as you experience hunger, sleepiness, and thirst, you need to experience the myriad of emotions inside you so that you can lose your coldness, distance, and isolation. My prayer for you is that God will help free you of the emotions you have stuffed inside yourself. May you be free

DISTANCE

to become that lively, vivacious person God created you to become.

Pink = Disconnected/Distant/Detached

Alone/Isolated/Abandoned – Accompanied

Hebrews 13:5 says, "I will never leave you nor forsake you." NKJV

Romans 8:38-39 says, "For I am convinced that neither death nor life, neither angels nor demons, neither the present nor the future, nor any powers, neither height nor depth, nor anything else in all creation, will be able to separate us from the love of God that is in Christ Jesus our Lord." NIV

Isaiah 49:15-16 says, "Can a mother forget the baby at her breast and have no compassion on the child she has borne? Though she may forget, I will not forget you! See, I have engraved you on the palms of my hands; your walls are ever before me." NIV

Psalm 27:10 says, "My father and mother walked out and left me, but God took me in." Message Bible. The NIV says, "Though my father and mother forsake me, the Lord will receive me."

Romans 8:37-39 says, "In all these things we are more than conquerors through Him who loved us. For I am convinced that neither death nor life, neither angels nor demons, neither the present nor the future, nor any powers, neither height nor depth, nor anything else in all creation, will be able to separate us from the love of God that is in Christ Jesus our Lord." NIV

DISTANCE

Distant/Detached/Indifferent/Aloof – Close/Connected/Friendly

Revelation 21:4 says, "He will wipe every tear from their eyes. There will be no more death or mourning or crying or pain, for the old order of things has passed away." NIV

Isaiah 25:8 says, "The Sovereign Lord will wipe away the tears from all faces." NIV

Matthew 5:4 says, "Blessed are those who morn, for they will be comforted." NIV

John 15:5 says, "I am the vine; you are the branches. If a man remains in me and I in him, he will bear much fruit; apart from Me you can do nothing." NIV

← 18 →

Hope

Have you ever felt hopeless? What caused those feelings? What happened when you felt hopeless? I can name what caused my feelings of hopelessness. It was my life. It felt dark, and the pain was so all-consuming. It hung over me thickly. Many aspects of my life weighed me down. Things seemed impossible. A way through these difficulties seemed almost nonexistent. I was surrounded by many seemingly unsurmountable challenges and had almost no friends or support. I felt alone, and despair was all around me.

Can you relate to these feelings? The voices of my past ripped into me, weighing me down. Can you relate? What things in your life lead to these feelings? What situations in your life weigh you down? What triggers cause these beliefs to permeate your mind?

It is time to stand up against these lies. It is time to say to this thinking and these situations in your life that you serve a mighty God—a God that tells you through Luke 1:37, "With Him, nothing is impossible."

God promises in Isaiah 61:3 that He will "Bestow on them a crown of beauty instead of ashes, the oil of joy instead of mourning, and a garment of praise instead of a spirit of despair." And Psalm 30:11, says, "You turned my wailing into dancing; you removed my sackcloth and clothed me with joy."

Do you believe this? It is time you proclaim this at the top of your lungs. Hope comes when you reach out to God.

HOPE

It comes when you begin tuning into His voice. It comes when you begin calling out to Him for help.

Recently, during my quiet time, the story of the Good Samaritan flooded my mind. A man is lying on the side of the road. I imagine that maybe he is bloody, parched, bruised, and too weak to move. People coming down the road step around him and ignore him. He is alone and hurting. The heat of the day is scorching his skin. He is so thirsty and feeling so hopeless, unloved, and so alone. Can you relate to this story? I know I can.

People continue to pass by, and the man is losing hope. He is becoming weaker and weaker. He cries out for help, "Father, help me." Suddenly, a form comes, lifts him in His arms, and carries him away to safety. In this place, this man is cared for. His wounds are cleaned, and he is given water, food, and a bed. The person who carries him away sits with him, holds his hands, talks to him, comforts him, and speaks life back into him. This good Samaritan is God, our Heavenly Father.

He is with you when no one else sees your pain, your shame, your resentments, your grief, your hopelessness, your loneliness, or your guilt. He aches to come alongside you to fill you with hope, love, peace, and comfort. Are you willing to let him? Turning to Him is where you will find hope.

Black = Suicidal Thoughts/Guilty

Guilt/Regret – Innocence/Shameless

> John 3:16-17 says, "For God so loved the world that He gave His one and only Son, that whoever believes in Him shall not perish but have eternal life. For God

HOPE

did not send His Son into the world to condemn the world, but to save the world through Him." NIV

Psalm 51:1-5,7 says, "Have mercy on me, O God, according to your unfailing love; according to your great compassion blot out my transgressions. Wash away all my iniquity and cleanse me from my sin. For I know my transgressions, and my sin is always before me. Against you, you only, have I sinned and done what is evil in your sight . . . Cleanse me with hyssop, and I will be clean; wash me, and I will be whiter than snow." NIV

Isaiah 1:18 says, "Come now, let us reason together," says the Lord, "Though your sins are like scarlet, they shall be as white as snow; though they are red as crimson, they shall be like wool." NIV

Loneliness – Friendships

Psalm 27:10 says, "When my father and my mother forsake me, then the Lord will take care of me." NKJV

Psalm 68:6 says, "God sets the solitary in families." NKJV

John 14:18 says, "I will not leave you orphans; I will come to you." NKJV

Melancholy/Depression/Sadness – Cheerful/ Happiness

Psalm 34:17 says, "The righteous cry out, and the Lord hears them; He delivers them from all their

HOPE

troubles. The Lord is close to the brokenhearted and saves those who are crushed in spirit." NIV

I Peter 5:7 says, "Cast all your anxiety on Him because He cares for you." NIV

Revelation 21:4 says, "He will wipe every tear from their eyes. There will be no more death or mourning or crying or pain, for the old order of things has passed away." NIV

Psalm 30:11 says, "He turned my wailing into dancing; you removed my sackcloth and clothed me with joy, that my heart may sing to you and not be silent." NIV

Psalm 147:3 says, "He heals the brokenhearted and binds up their wounds." NIV

Hopeless/Despair – Hope

Jeremiah 29:11 says, "'For I know the plans I have for you,'" declares the Lord. 'Plans to prosper you and not to harm you; plans to give you hope and a future.'" NIV

I Corinthians 10:13 says, "No trial has overtaken you that is not faced by others. And God is faithful: He will not let you be tried beyond what you are able to bear, but with the trial will also provide a way out so that you may be able to endure it." NET

Luke 1:37 says, "For with God nothing will be impossible." NKJV

HOPE

Romans 15:13 says, "May the God of hope fill you with all joy and peace as you trust in Him, so that you may overflow with hope by the power of the Holy Spirit." NIV

← 19 →

Stress and Worry

Life creates burdens and stress. I don't know what you are facing today, but I do know that God aches to help you with your stress.

I know no better way to reduce stress and worry than to sing. As I think about this I am reminded of the slaves. Often, they were heard singing as they worked to serve their masters. Their voices lifted up among the trials and difficulties of their lives. We owe so many beautiful songs to these men and women who composed them during the struggles and difficulties they faced.

Many hymns were composed out of trials and difficulties. I love hymns as they have so much meat and meaning to them. Many excellent hymns provide us with the courage we need to face the difficulties that we experience in our lives. I have enclosed a few of the hymns that I love. These are the ones I turn to for strength. I love playing them on the piano and singing to them. They fill me with encouragement. So many hymns exist, and I encourage each of you to find ones that you enjoy. Use them to help you when you are facing difficulties and need encouragement.

STRESS AND WORRY

What a Friend We Have in Jesus

What a friend we have in Jesus,
All our sins and griefs to bear;
What a privilege to carry
Everything to God in prayer!
O what peace we often forfeit,
O what needless pain we bear,
All because we do not carry
Everything to God in prayer.

Have we trials and temptations?
Is there trouble anywhere?
We should never be discouraged;
Take it to the Lord in prayer!
Can we find a friend so faithful,
Who will all our sorrows share?
Jesus knows our every weakness;
Take it to the Lord in prayer!

Are we weak and heavy laden,
Cumbered with a load of care?
Precious Savior, still our refuge,
Take it to the Lord in prayer!
Do thy friends despise, forsake thee?
Take it to the Lord in prayer!
In His arms He'll take and shield thee,
Thou wild find a solace there.

Joseph Scriven[1]

STRESS AND WORRY

Turn Your Eyes Upon Jesus

O soul, are you weary and troubled?
No light in the darkness you see?
There's light for a look at the Savior,
And life more abundant and free!

Turn your eyes upon Jesus,
Look full in His wonderful face;
And the things of earth
Will grow strangely dim
In the light of His glory and grace.

Through death into life everlasting
He passed, and we follow Him there;
Over us sin no more hath dominion,
For more than conqu'rors we are!

Turn your eyes upon Jesus,
Look full in His wonderful face;
And the things of earth
Will grow strangely dim
In the light of His glory and grace.

His word shall not fail you He promised;
Believe Him and all will be well:
Then go to a world that is dying,
His perfect salvation to tell!

STRESS AND WORRY

Turn your eyes upon Jesus,
Look full in His wonderful face;
And the things of earth
Will grow strangely dim
In the light of His glory and grace.

Helen Lemmel[2]

STRESS AND WORRY

Showers of Blessings

"There shall be showers of blessings;"
This is the promise of love;
There shall be seasons refreshing,
Sent from the Savior above.

Showers of blessing,
Showers of blessing we need;
Mercy drops round us are falling,
But for the showers we plead.

"There shall be showers of blessing–"
Precious reviving again;
Over the hills and the valleys,
Sound of abundance of rain,

Showers of blessing,
Showers of blessing we need;
Mercy drops round us are falling,
But for the showers we plead.

"There shall be showers of blessing;"
Send them upon us, O Lord;
Grant to us now a refreshing;
Come, and now honor Thy word,

Showers of blessing,
Showers of blessing we need;
Mercy drops round us are falling,
But for the showers we plead.

STRESS AND WORRY

"There shall be showers of blessing;"
O that today they might fall,
Now as to God we're confessing,
Now as on Jesus we call!

Showers, of blessing,
Showers of blessing we need;
Mercy drops round us are falling,
But for the showers we plead.

Daniel Whittle[3]

STRESS AND WORRY

Sweet Hour of Prayer

Sweet hour of prayer, sweet hour of player,
That calls me from a world of care,
And bids me, at my Father's throne,
Make all my wants and wishes known!
In seasons of distress and grief,
My souls has often found relief,
And oft escaped the tempters snare,
By they return, sweet hour of prayer.

Sweet hour of prayer! Sweet hour of prayer!
Thy wings shall my petition bear
To Him whose truth and faithfulness
Engage the waiting soul to bless.
And since He bids me seek His face,
Believe His word, and trust His grace,
I'll cast on Him my every care,
And wait for thee, sweet hour of prayer.

Sweet hour of prayer! Sweet hour of prayer!
May I thy consolation share
Till from Mount Pisgah's lofty height
I view my home and take my flight.
In my immortal flesh I'll rise
To seize the everlasting prize.
And shout while passing through the air,
"Farewell, farewell, sweet hour of prayer!"

William Walford[4]

STRESS AND WORRY

I Must Tell Jesus

I must tell Jesus all of my trials;
I cannot bear these burdens alone,
In my distress He kindly will help me,
He ever loves and cares for His own.

I must tell Jesus! I must tell Jesus!
I cannot bear my burdens alone;
I must tell Jesus! I must tell Jesus!
Jesus can help me, Jesus alone.

I must tell Jesus all of my troubles,
He is a kind, compassionate Friend;
If I but ask Him, He will deliver,
Makes of my troubles quickly an end.

I must tell Jesus! I must tell Jesus!
I cannot bear my burdens alone;
I must tell Jesus! I must tell Jesus!
Jesus can help me, Jesus alone.

O how the world to evil allures me!
O how my heart is tempted to sin!
I must tell Jesus, and He will help me
Over the world the vict'ry win.

I must tell Jesus! I must tell Jesus!
I cannot bear my burdens alone;
I must tell Jesus! I must tell Jesus!
Jesus can help me, Jesus alone.

Elisha Hoffman[5]

STRESS AND WORRY

He Leadeth Me

He leadeth me! O blessed thought!
O words with heavenly comfort fraught!
Whate'er I do, whe'er I be,
Still 'tis God's hand that leadeth me.

He leadeth me, He leadeth me,
By His own hand He leadeth me;
His faithful follower I would be,
For by His hand He leadeth me.

Sometimes 'mid scenes of deepest gloom,
Sometimes where Eden's bowers bloom,
By waters still, o'er troubled sea
Still 'tis His hand that leadeth me!

He leadeth me, He leadeth me,
By His own hand He leadeth me;
His faithful follower I would be,
For by His hand He leadeth me.

Lord, I would clasp my hand in Thine,
Nor ever murmur nor repine;
Content, whatever lot I see,
Since 'tis my God that leadeth me.

He leadeth me, He leadeth me,
By His own hand He leadeth me;
His faithful follower I would be,
For by His hand He leadeth me.

STRESS AND WORRY

And when my task on earth is done,
When, by the grace, the victory's won,
E'en death's cold wave I will not flee,
Since God through Jordan leadeth me.

He leadeth me, He leadeth me,
By His own hand He leadeth me;
His faithful follower I would be,
For by His hand He leadeth me.

Joseph Gilmore[6]

STRESS AND WORRY

Abide With Me

Abide with me;
Fast falls the even tide;
The darkness deepens;
Lord, with me abide!
When other helpers
Fail, and comforts flee,
Help of the helpless,
O abide with me!

Swift to its close ebbs
Out life's little day;
Earth's joys grow dim,
It's glories pass away;
Change and decay
In all around I see;
O though, who changest not,
Abide with me!

I need Thy presence
Every passing hour;
What but Thy grace
Can foil the tempter's power?
Who like Thyself
My guide and stay can be?
Through cloud and sunshine,
O abide with me!

I fear no foe,
With Thee at hand to bless;
Ills have no weight,
And tears no bitterness:

STRESS AND WORRY

Where is death's sting?
Where, grave, thy victory?
I triumph still
If Thou abide with me!

Henry Lyte[7]

Grey = Stressed, Exhausted, Worry, Overwhelmed, Impossible

Burdened/Weighed Down – Peace, Calm, Serenity

Psalm 55:22 says, "Cast your cares on the Lord and He will sustain you; He will never let the righteous fall." NIV

Philippians 4:13 says, "I can do everything through Him who gives me strength." NIV

Isaiah 41:10 says, "So do not fear, for I am with you; do not be dismayed, for I am your God. I will strengthen you and help you; I will uphold you with my righteous right hand." NIV

Habakkuk 3:19 says, "The Lord God is my strength; He will make my feet like deer's feet, and He will make me walk on my high hills." NKJV

Exhausted/Frazzled/Drained – Invigorated/Rested/ Refreshed

Isaiah 40:31 says, "But they who wait for the Lord shall renew their strength; they shall mount up with wings like eagles, they shall run and not be weary, they shall walk and not be faint." NKJV

Matthew 11:28-30 says, "Come to me, all you who are weary and burdened, and I will give you rest. Take my yoke upon you and learn from me, for I am gentle and humble in heart, and you will find rest for your souls. For my yoke is easy and my burden is light." NIV

Mark 6:31 says, "Come to Me by yourselves to a quiet place and get some rest." NIV

Exodus 33:14 says, "My presence will go with you, and I will give you rest." NIV

Impossible – Possible

Psalm 34:17 says, "The righteous cry out, and the Lord hears them; He delivers them from all their troubles." NIV

Matthew 19:26 says, "With men this is impossible, but with God all things are possible." NKJV

Philippians 4:13 says, "I can do all things through Christ who strengthens me." NKJV

Lacking (financially, wisdom, etc.) – Provided For

Philippians 4:19 says, "And my God will meet all your needs according to His glorious riches in Christ Jesus." NIV

James 1:5 says, "If any of you lacks wisdom, he should ask God, who gives generously to all without finding fault, and it will be given to him." NIV

STRESS AND WORRY

John 6:11-12 says, "Jesus then took the loaves, gave thanks, and distributed to those who were seated as much as they wanted." NIV

Genesis 21:19 says, "Then God opened her eyes and she saw a well of water. So she went and filled the skin with water and gave the boy a drink." NIV

Psalm 119:18 says, "Open my eyes that I may see . . ." NIV

Overwhelmed – Peaceful

Isaiah 26:3-4 says, "You keep him in perfect peace, whose mind is stayed on you, because he trusts in you. Trust in the Lord forever, for in Yah, the Lord, is everlasting strength." NKJV

John 14:1 Jesus says, "Do not let your hearts be troubled. Trust in God; trust also in me." NIV

Psalm 28:7 says, "The Lord is my strength and my shield; my heart trusts in Him, and I am helped. My heart leaps for joy and I will give thanks to Him in song." NIV

Mathew 6:34 says, "Therefore do not be worry about tomorrow, for tomorrow will worry about itself. Each day has enough trouble of its own." NIV

Uptight – Relaxed

Matthew 11:28-30 says, "Are you tired? Worn out? Burned out on religion? Come to me. Get away with me and you'll recover your life. I'll show you how to take a real rest. Walk with me and work with

STRESS AND WORRY

me—watch how I do it. Learn the unforced rhythms of grace. I won't lay anything heavy or ill-fitting on you. Keep company with me and you'll learn to live freely and lightly." Message Bible

Psalm 27:1 says, "The Lord is my light and my salvation—whom shall I fear? The Lord is the stronghold of my life—of whom shall I be afraid?" NIV

Psalm 61:1-2 says, "Hear my cry, O God; listen to my prayer. From the ends of the earth I call to you, I call as my heart grows faint; lead me to the rock that is higher than I." NIV

Isaiah 41:10 says, "Don't panic. I'm with you. There's no need to fear for I'm your God. I'll give you strength. I'll help you. I'll hold you steady, keep a firm grip on you." Message Bible

Weary/Worn Out – Energized

Isaiah 40:31 says, "But those who wait upon God get fresh strength. They spread their wings and soar like eagles, they run and don't get tired, they walk and don't lag behind." Message Bible

Matthew 11:28-30 says, "Come to me all who are weary and heavy laden, and I will give you rest. Take my yoke upon you and learn from Me, for I am gentle and lowly in heart, and you will find rest for your souls. For my yoke is easy and My burden is light." NKJV

STRESS AND WORRY

Proverbs 11:25 says, "A generous soul will prosper, and he who refreshes others will himself be refreshed." BSB

Worried – <mark>Reassured/Trust</mark>

Philippians 4:6-7 says, "Don't fret or worry. Instead of worrying, pray. Let petitions and praises shape your worries into prayers, letting God know your concerns. Before you know it, a sense of God's wholeness, everything coming together for good, will come and settle you down. It's wonderful what happens when Christ displaces worry at the center of your life." Message Bible

I Corinthians 10:13 says, "No trial or temptation has seized you except what is common to man. And God is faithful; He will not let you be tempted beyond what you can bear. But when you are tempted, He will also provide a way out so that you can stand up under it." NIV

Matthew 6:27-28 says, "Can all your worries add a single moment to your life? And why worry about your clothing? Look at the lilies of the field and how they grow. They don't work to make their clothing, yet Solomon in all his glory was not dressed as beautifully as they are. And if God cares so wonderfully for wildflowers that are here today and thrown into the fire tomorrow, He will certainly care for you. Why do you have so little faith?" NLT

Matthew 6:34 says, "So don't worry about tomorrow, for tomorrow will bring its own worries. Today's trouble is enough for today." NLT

STRESS AND WORRY

Prayer for you: Heavenly Father, help me put my trust in you. Remove all the lies I have been taught from my past. Replace these lies with your truth. Satan, enough is enough. I will no longer believe these lies. God tells me I am worthy. God tells me that nothing is impossible with Him. Today, Father, I ask that as my Great Physician that you will do the work inside of me to change me on the inside. Help me believe the truth of your word. I am a child of God. I belong to you. I am loved by you. Nothing at all can separate me from your love. Help me to trust you. Help me to remember that you will cleanse me as white as snow when I come to you in repentance. Father, today I ask that you will help me hear your voice loud and clear. I want to be filled with your love, joy, peace, goodness, serenity, happiness, worthiness, kindness, calmness, gentleness, self-control, and humility. Wash me, Father, and make me white as snow.

Help me believe that I am clean, that I am worthy, that I am appreciated, loved, and accepted. Thank you, Father, for the healing you have done in my life. Thank you for dying for me on the cross. Thank you for loving me, sin and all, and for never giving up on me. Thank you for helping me see your truth. Thank you for defeating the lies of my past and for making me new inside and out. I praise you, Father, because of your goodness, love, and mercy. Thank you for being my great healer, my comforter, my restorer, my king, my provider, and my teacher. And Father, thank you for bringing beauty out of ashes and for taking my mess and giving me a message and for taking my tests and giving me a testimony. Amen.

References

1. Scriven, Joseph. "What a Friend We Have in Jesus"
2. Lemmel, Helen. "Turn Your Eyes Upon Jesus"
3. Whittle, Daniel. "Showers of Blessing"
4. Walford, William. "Sweet Hour of Prayer"
5. Hoffman, Elisha. "I Must Tell Jesus"
6. Gilmore, Joseph. "He Leadeth Me"
7. Lyte, Henry. "Abide With Me: Fast Falls the Even Tide"

Free Material

Affirmations are truths that help change the way we think. By placing these positive thoughts in our minds we can begin to counter the negative thoughts and negative things we say to ourselves. You can claim fifty Bible affirmations by going to the link found at:
https://godsaffirmations.com/affirmations.

Thank You

Thank you for reading this book. I would appreciate it if you would leave your honest review on Amazon. If you leave less than five stars—please tell me how I can improve my book. If you leave five stars and wish you could leave more—please tell the world.

www.ingramcontent.com/pod-product-compliance
Lightning Source LLC
Chambersburg PA
CBHW050248120526
44590CB00016B/2268